Black Paper 1977

Edited by
C.B.Cox and Rhodes Boyson

Temple Smith · London

First published in Great Britain 1977
by Maurice Temple Smith Ltd
37 Great Russell Street, London WC1

ISBN 0 85117 1176

Photoset and printed Photolitho
in Great Britain by
Ebenezer Baylis & Son Ltd
The Trinity Press, Worcester, and London

Contents

3 VALUES

concern abt stnds not only in this cntry but in Eur. + N. Am, hve. there's useless now for a back to basics movement.

Sometimes, Mr. B. gets his quotings mixed up. A review by Woodrow Wyatt, wh appeared in T Sun. Times, is attrib. to T Obs. ———, we are not normally told t ——— orientation o t pple quoted. who, f e.g., is C. H. Lawrence, whose somethings in T Times are awarded '1? pse o quotation.

There are some clues to t editors' order o priorities: 'It is vital in study educ tt both t ——— avail., nthing ft intellect. gifted e a good gen. educ for t avail. very able snd. survive.' (my italics)

~~T ———— ct selections we find language. Tcls, prop. t develop o specialised ———— etc. Some ———, ——, some ———— ———~~

It is characteristic o t blank Papers tt Mr. Baldwin deplores a ——— badly significant decline in ——— O e A level exam nrecory, tries to attrib. it to t new structures o study educ. but sys. nothing abt t content or t value o exam sys. as presently taught. Baldwin, however, at least deserves regard for his careful sifting o stats. But he doesn't convince. There may be all sorts o reasons for t ——— lower performance o ———. Their ——— may be ———. There may be more o them in ——/——— areas.

Letter to Members of Parliament

In April 1969, Mr Short, then Secretary of State for Education and Science, said that the publication of the *Black Paper* was one of the blackest days for education for 100 years. He described our criticism of informal education as 'archaic rubbish'. In October 1976, Mr Callaghan, the Prime Minister, attempted to steal our clothes, which have always been freely available. He repeated our assertions that money is being wasted, standards are too low, and children are not being given the basic tools of literacy and numeracy. *The Times Educational Supplement* said of Mr Callaghan's speech: 'He has gathered his Black Paper cloak around him.'

Why has this apparent change of heart taken place? In 1969 the contributors to the *Black Papers* were treated with abuse and contempt, but their stand gave heart to many teachers who knew from their own experience that informal methods were not working. As the years passed by, the evidence that standards were declining became overwhelming.

In this *Black Paper* Mr Alfred Levy gives details of simple arithmetic tests which were beyond the ability of the majority of the first year at his comprehensive (pp. 23–29). On 20 October 1976, it was reported that at St John's Comprehensive School, Newham, London, about a quarter of the 135 children who entered from the primary school needed special help with reading. Children of average ability aged 14 to 16 needed basic lessons in fractions and decimals, and made elementary errors in English, such as starting a sentence without a capital letter and making simple spelling mistakes. This school is *not* unusual; such reports are now common. The problem at St John's with reading standards of primary school children should be compared with the successes of Mr Beard (of Tameside fame) in his traditional school, described on pp. 42–43; such standards were usual in the 1930s. In this *Black Paper* we give details of recent research projects which demonstrate that formal methods achieve the best results in training children to be literate and numerate. Our case is now accepted by all except the fanatical devotees of progressive education, who unfortunately still retain too much power in schools and colleges. As Mr Callaghan pointed out, we now spend six billion pounds a year on education, a huge increase over the 1930s in its share of the gross national product as well as in gross terms. With all this increased expenditure should not standards have obviously and markedly risen? The fact that they have declined proves how disastrously informal teaching has affected our schools. Dolly Walker's description of the goings-on at William Tyndale shows why standards are tumbling. Personal contact with schools of this kind was one reason why the *Black Paper* editors began their campaign in 1969.

Even after Mr Callaghan's speech, progressives still claim that standards are rising. They point out that the number of children passing O- and A-levels has considerably increased since 1960. The reason for this, of course, is that so many more children are staying on at school and taking these examinations, in which the same approximate percentage always pass. The standards are not objective. What is really happening was forcibly described by an experienced A-level examiner on 25 October 1976:

> In recent years the number of very weak candidates taking A-levels has grown considerably. I have myself heard teachers speak of this as the deliberate policy of their schools, intended to lower the standards so that more passes can be gained, and more of their pupils be placed in the higher grades. What makes this aim possible is that, by request of the Schools Council, the number of candidates in each grade does not fall below a certain minimum proportion of the total entry, whatever the marks given. When I see where my own average mark now lies, I cannot doubt that these schools have gained their objective.
>
> What alarms me more is that few even of the ablest candidates can express themselves as clearly and accurately as the average run of candidates could do 17 years ago. This deterioration is not reflected in the marks given. The task of an examiner is to discriminate, as justly as he can, between the various scripts that lie before him, and in order that the semi-literate but quite intelligent and well-informed candidate may be adequately distinguished from others of lower calibre it is necessary to give the former quite high marks. What determines the mark is thus to a large extent the fact that so few candidates are better, and so many are much worse.
>
> 'Semi-literate' is not too strong a word. Slips are, of course, natural in examination conditions, but these were the same in past years, when only a handful of candidates wrote as the majority now do. It may sound of little importance that some candidates cannot spell such simple words as 'sister', 'writing', 'women', 'better' and 'whom'; that paucity of vocabulary leads to such coinages as 'oldness' and 'magiclike'; that malapropisms like 'indignity' (for indignation) and 'eminent' (for imminent) appear in script after script. In fact the cumulative effect of dozens of such errors in a single script is considerable. Understanding is hindered when a piece of work has to be not merely read but translated. Nor is it always possible to discern what word the writer intended. I am still baffled by 'cronical'. Chronicle? Chronic? Comical? Inevitably the candidates' own powers of comprehension are also reduced, as was strikingly illustrated a few years ago when a question was set containing the word 'momentous'; candidates who assumed this to mean 'momentary' were obviously at a disadvantage.
>
> *Daily Telegraph*

Why are standards so low? The reason is a breakdown in teaching, and it is time the NUT stopped pretending otherwise. What is happening is made abundantly clear in an article by Peter Medway, head of English, Crofton High School, Wakefield.

Mr Medway argues that we should accept 'unorthodox spelling':

> So am I advocating a lowering of standards? Yes. We've lowered standards of Latin for university entrance, of property holding for voting, of 'standard English' for broadcasting. Let spelling standards be the next: they are wasteful and irrelevant, and they are used to put people down and make them feel inadequate. The freelances who see the quest for perfect spelling as an absurd rigmarole have basically got it right. If education means filling your head with nonsense about 'decide' not 'dicide', I for one can't blame them if they dicide it's not for them.
>
> *The Times Educational Supplement*, 28 May 1976.

With teachers like Mr Medway it is not surprising that able young people use words such as 'cronical', and cannot tell the difference between 'momentary' and 'momentous'.

Mr Callaghan will find his proposals for a return to basics vigorously resisted by local advisers and inspectors. The head-mistress of a London school in a working-class area took over in 1974 when it had a serious reading problem at the leaving age. This was dealt with by tackling it from the earliest age, as Mr Beard might have done, and there was great improvement. But an inspector called and was outraged at the lack of play facilities, and because some of the under-fives were actually learning to read. In Manchester in a working-class area an enthusiastic teacher devoted herself to teaching all her six-year-olds to begin reading. An adviser called, and spent the day with the children. At the end of the afternoon the adviser said to the teacher: 'All your children can read. You have obviously spent far too much time on the teaching of reading.'

These bad ideas come from the Plowden Report, which declared that 'finding out' has proved better for children than 'being told', and that the 'distinction between work and play is false, possibly throughout life, certainly in primary school'. The headmaster of Bedford Modern School wrote on 26 October 1976: 'those in the educational world are well aware how such unqualified pronouncements have been hammered into young students in colleges of education, who have been told that they must never face a class or teach in the traditional manner, but *all* primary school work must be on the informal basis.' Until teachers realise the falsity of these notions there will be no major improvement in educational standards.

Mrs Shirley Williams donned a *Black Paper* hat when she declared that large comprehensives had proved unsuccessful. For political reasons Mr Callaghan avoided this issue. The *Black Paper* arguments against comprehensives have always been based on practical reasons why these schools in many circumstances, though not in all, cannot succeed in maintaining standards. In this *Black Paper* we quote Iris Murdoch and Jacquetta Hawkes, both well-known Labour Party supporters, arguing that a comprehensive system damages the chances of the able working-class child. It is urgent that the Labour Party should face this problem, and no longer shuffle it aside for reasons of political expediency.

We hope that the likelihood of educational cuts at a time of economic crisis leads not to a battle to defend existing empires but to a complete re-assessment of priorities. We are glad that the Labour Party, which as recently as 1975 attacked our ideas so viciously, is now admitting the need for some of our reforms: the sooner they support all our proposals, the better it will be for the children of this country. The test of Mr Callaghan's and the Labour Party's conversion will be whether they are really prepared to take action to enforce standards and judge schools as teaching institutions. Our recommendations are summarised below.

School standards

We suggest the return of the national inspectorate of HMIs to their original task of the inspection of schools. At the same time the national monitoring of basic standards by examinations for all children at the ages of 7, 11 and 14 or 15 should be introduced. The school results of these tests should be available to parents, school governors and the local community. Children's names should not be published, but parents have a right to know the comparative achievements of schools. Schools which fall below standard should be investigated. There is no moral justification for compulsory education without the state guaranteeing and enforcing minimum standards. The 14 plus or 15 plus examination could be used as a leaving examination, and should test basic literacy and numeracy and a body of knowledge we should expect all our citizens to acquire. This is the genuine core curriculum for which Mr Callaghan asks. Once unemployment declines, pupils should be allowed to leave if they so choose when they pass the examination. If they fail they must return to school and sit it again at 16. This would do more for basic literacy and numeracy than 1,000 courses and 50,000 more teachers. Recent figures of juvenile unemployment are alarming, but much of it will remain as long as schools allow illiterates to leave at 16, many of whom have played truant for one or two years and in their attitudes are almost unemployable.

While teachers should be free to teach by any reasonable method provided they obtain good results, it should be made clear that all the evidence is that, on the average, informal non-structured classrooms attain far lower standards than formal structured traditional classrooms. Children should no longer be used as guinea pigs for untried and generally ineffective methods. New methods should only be tried in one or two specially designated experimental schools maintained by each authority. The children in these schools should be chosen only with parental consent; the teachers should be specially trained and the results carefully monitored and published.

Teachers

We suggest that there should be more emphasis on the quality of teachers accepted for training, and that standards of entry to the profession should be raised. We suggest that teacher-trainees spend their first year in schools apprenticed to a 'master-teacher' who would be appropriately rewarded for this responsibility. Teacher-trainees who are then thought suitable should spend no more than two years on subject study at colleges of education. Graduate trainees similarly should spend one full year in a school before taking a three-month course at a Department of Education.

It is also essential that the number of teacher-trainees accepted should bear a direct relationship to the future number of teachers we are likely to be able to afford to employ. A pool of unemployed young teachers is of advantage to no one.

Secondary school organisation

The comparative results of comprehensive schools should be nationally monitored and published, and compared with results from the bipartite system with regard to basic numeracy and literacy, O- and A-levels, CSE results, attendance, juvenile delinquency, and staff turnover. If such results indicate that the comprehensive schools are less effective in any area then local education authorities should be encouraged to diversify their secondary school provision. Each school should be encouraged to develop a subject speciality. Special academic schools could be reintroduced for some 20–40 per cent of children, and large schools broken up. In all cases there should be careful provision for flexible interchange between schools for children who develop late.

The possibilities for parental choice of secondary (and primary) schools should be improved via the educational voucher or some other method. Schools that few wish to attend should be closed and their staff dispersed. The building could be reopened by a young head, a church or some other body capable of developing a school responsive to parental demand. In these times of conflicting values, conscript schools are less and less suited to the wishes of parents. Selection at 14, middle schools and sixth-form colleges are likely only to be temporary and ineffective palliatives for declining standards. The direct grant schools should be reabsorbed into the state system and used as super-selective academic schools to keep scholarship alive and show the standards possible with bright children.

Higher education

In higher education research facilities should be increasingly concentrated in certain specified universities, to which all university teachers should have easy access. There should be no further significant university expansion. Polytechnics should return to the purpose for which they were originally intended: first degree institutions for vocations in science, engineering, the professions and business. Their arts and social science departments should be cut back. With the present shortage of money a system of student loans rather than grants seems inevitable. Whatever scheme is adopted, it is essential that scholarships should be available in sufficient numbers to attract able working-class children to university and to stimulate high standards.

THE EDITORS

1
Informal
education

Background

Scratch a progressive and you find an ideologist.

LORD ANNAN, *August 1976.*

Now while I was gazing upon all these things, I turned my head to look back, and saw *Ignorance* come up to the River side: but he soon got over, and that without half that difficulty which the other two men met with. For it happened that there was then in that place one *Vain-hope*, a ferry-man, that with his boat helped him over: so he as the other I saw, did ascend the Hill to come up to the gate, only he came alone; neither did any man meet him with the least encouragement. When he was come up to the gate, he looked up to the writing that was above; and then began to knock supposing that entrance should have been quickly administered to him: But he was asked by the men that looked over the top of the gate, Whence came you? and what would you have? He answered, I have eat and drank in the presence of the king, and he has taught in our streets. Then they asked him for his certificate, that he might go in and shew it to the king. So he fumbled in his bosom for one, and found none. Then said they, have you none? But the man answered never a word.

JOHN BUNYAN

Since Black Paper 1975

The leaders of progressive education combine good intentions with ignorance and vain hope. In 1976 they received two body blows, the William Tyndale scandal and the Lancaster Bennett Report, which demonstrated the superiority of formal to informal teaching. The progressive reaction to Bennett was to seek desperately and unavailingly for flaws in his statistics, or to pretend that his conclusions were of limited importance. Professor Maurice Peston, once special adviser to Mr Prentice, was typically muddled in an article he wrote in *The Times Educational Supplement* on 3 September 1976. Progressive teachers, he said, 'may be mistaken, as may the whole of the Plowden Committee have been, but they deserve more serious criticism and analysis than is contained in one piece of research and one report on one school'.

The implication is that before Bennett and Tyndale there had been no serious criticism of progressive education. The sleight of hand by which this idea is slipped into an unwary reader's mind is typical of Professor Peston's style. Is he really so ignorant?

Attacks on progressive education, particularly in America by well-known writers such as Hannah Arendt and Jacques Barzun, were published even before the Plowden Report (1967). In 1969 Professor Peters's *Perspectives on Plowden* gathered together some excellent critical essays, and of course also in 1969 there were the first *Black Papers*.

Bennett's Report is only one of many pieces of research which show the superiority of formal teaching. In *The Times Educational Supplement* of 4 June 1976, he said he had located 'six studies of this sort, and they all show the same pattern. In one American study the high-ability children were one year and three months advanced in formal situations.' Some of these studies are unpublished conference papers; others are discussed below.

William Tyndale in Islington is not unique. A breakdown of sound learning has occurred in numerous British schools. The evidence of declining standards is now so overwhelming that even the Labour Party shows signs of wanting to take some action.

Research

Dr Bennett has himself pointed out that previous research, such as the NFER Report *The Roots of Reading* (Cane and Smithers), produced almost identical results to his own, but attracted little publicity at the time. This failure by a ruling Establishment to react to new research is a typical phenomenon; only gradually, particularly because of the publicity achieved by the *Black Papers*, have the progressives become aware that their ideas do not work in practice. Many progressives have claimed that the Bennett Report does not substantiate the claims made by the *Black Papers*. It obviously does. Perhaps it does not support the myth about the *Black Papers* put about by papers such as the *Guardian* or the *New Statesman*, that we want to put back the clock to the 1930s. Bennett's research does support our demand for the best of both formal and informal methods, for more structure and teacher direction in schools.

Jerome Bruner

The Bennett Report demonstrated that, within the space of a single school year, formally taught pupils at the top of the junior school shot ahead by the equivalent of three to four months in reading age. In mathematics the gap achieved was four to five months, in English, three to four months. Pupils in progressive schools did not surpass the formally taught children in creative story-writing. There was evidence that bright, anxious, insecure children were particularly harmed by informal teaching.

Professor Jerome Bruner, famous for his advocacy of discovery methods, reviewed the Bennett Report in *New Society* (29 April 1976). Like Dr Spock, Bruner has revised his opinions during the last decade. He praises the dispassionate skill with which Bennett combines conceptual subtlety with empirical open-mindedness, and continues:

> The main findings can be summed up quickly. The more formal the teaching, the more time pupils spend working on the subject matter at hand. And in general—though with some important exceptions—the more time pupils spend working on a subject, the more they improve at it—not a huge surprise, but one that grows in importance as one looks at the other results. For though it may come as no revelation that students in the more formal classrooms improved considerably more in reading and in mathematical skills than the less formally taught, it is much more revealing that pupils in informal settings did *not* do any better on their creative writing than their more formally instructed fellows.

The results include some minor discrepancies, and, as Bennett has repeatedly urged, his research does not signal the end of informal teaching. However, significant changes in cultural attitudes have occurred since the late 1960s. Bruner writes:

> We are just at the end of an era in the human sciences in which concepts of self-direction, self-realisation and self-reward lived unchallenged in a world where self-determination was the ideal. And indeed, this ideal is central to the democratic concept. But ends and means become confused: what of self-demand feeding schedules for babies? What of the 'innateness hypothesis', in whose name it was insisted that language is discovered and need not be taught? And what of the ever more dominating contemporary cultures of youth? The adult as model or teacher or friend is in eclipse. Common sense and technical inquiry are finally catching up with the romantic excess. It turns out that the mother and her reactions are crucial for language acquisition and that self-demand in feeding and infant care leaves the child without a stable source of reciprocation. New studies are now pointing to the critical role of the adult tutor, in social and intellectual development. Early connection with a supporting world begins to emerge as a *leitmotif* for the development of later self-determination. And, indeed, one of the central issues is to assure the dispossessed that this connection is not destroyed by isolating alienation.

Bruner's emphasis on 'a supporting role' is very close to Hannah Arendt's arguments of twenty years ago (see p. 92). Many writers now think of the 1960s as a disastrous period for the Western world, in which ill-thought-out notions of spontaneity, self-realisation and equality invaded both education and the Arts. Professor Donald Davie, poet and critic, recently drew attention to the breakdown of order and proportion in the 1960s, 'that hideous decade'. In the 1970s, we are witnessing a slow return to common sense, to formal teaching, to a renewed awareness that the child's happiness and personal fulfilment depend on a secure environment under the control of adults.

Research on progressive teaching often includes anomalies. High standards can be achieved by one exceptionally able informal teacher, as in the Bennett survey. But for the average classroom the importance of formal teaching is now well established by recent research. Here are some examples, which presumably Professor Peston has not read:

Learning to read: The Great Debate, by Dr Jeanne Chall, 1967. We dealt with this in *Black*

Paper 1975. Dr Chall, a professor at Harvard, analysed studies comparing different approaches to beginning reading, and also observed how reading was taught in over 300 classrooms in the US, England and Scotland. Her conclusion was that research 'does not support the prevailing view that sees the beginning reader as a miniature adult who should, from the start, engage in mature reading'. There should be early stress on code learning, and this involves teacher direction and control. The whole-word approach was inferior to a phonics approach. This major book (oddly not even mentioned in the Bullock Report) is in tune with research in England undertaken by Dr Joyce Morris, and this too we have dealt with in previous *Black Papers.*

The Roots of Reading, by Brian Cane and Jane Smithers, 1971. This was described at length by Stuart Froome in *Black Paper 1975*, and was also not mentioned in the Bullock Report. Here are the main conclusions:

Apart from having noisier surroundings, the unsuccessful schools did, in general, stand out as a group. The major difference—and it is one which forms a theme running through our findings—was the lack of systematic instruction in the unsuccessful schools. There was considerable neglect of phonics (the sounds of individual letters and combinations of letters). There were few set periods of reading instruction, and in many classrooms the teachers waited for the children to manifest some interest in reading spontaneously before they attended to this subject. In the successful schools, reading instruction tended to be organised and recognisable from the start, and early phonic instruction was common. Although there was more permissiveness in the unsuccessful schools, relations between teachers and children were informal in most schools of both kinds. What distinguished the two groups of schools were not the warmth of atmosphere, nor the degree of concern for the children, which was manifest in most classrooms, but rather the extent to which the teacher exerted direct control over the children's learning. The unsuccessful schools favoured activity methods and creative work *at the expense of* organised learning.

It should be noted well that there were excep-

tions to this norm, and that the most successful school of all (Godwin) was one which combined activity methods and creativity with a certain amount of teacher-direction, especially in organising the learning of phonics.

The atmosphere in the successful schools, which was often strongly influenced by the headmasters' attitudes, was usually firmer and less indulgent than in the unsuccessful schools, but not to the extent of being harshly authoritarian. Relations between head and teachers were generally more formal in these schools, and relations with parents more remote and excluding. The more permissive attitude in the unsuccessful schools, however, was rather ambiguous. While appearing to display more 'sympathy' for the children and their home backgrounds, some of the teachers tended to be condescending in their attitudes, and may well have underestimated the abilities of their pupils. This would have depressed the children's achievement.

As in Bennett, there is an exception, but the superiority of formal teaching in the usual classroom situation is made abundantly clear.

'Reading Achievement and Creativity as Related to Open Classroom Experience', by William D. Ward and Peter R. Barcher, *Journal of Educational Psychology*, 1975. This is a small piece of research based on 49 children matched on IQ, socioeconomic status, sex, age and grade with 49 subjects from classrooms identified as traditional. The summary concludes: 'Among low IQ groups, open and traditional subjects could not be distinguished on reading achievement or creativity. Among high IQ children, traditional subjects had significantly higher reading and figural creativity scores.'

In the subsequent article, Ward and Barcher tell us that 'among the high IQ groups, the open children achieved a level commensurate with the national norms, and the traditional subjects were over a year advanced.'

'Helping Children to Read,' by Carole Striker, *New Society*, 5 February 1976. This is also a small-scale study, carried out at the Department of Psychology, University of Keele, and based on 80 poor readers between 10 and 11 years old, in their last year at primary school. The children were all from families in which the parents had manual occupations, and little reading was done at home by either parents or children. There were 43 boys and 37 girls. Experienced teachers took an 'interest' group and a 'skill' group, and the progress of the two was compared. The interest group started from the child's own experience, football, or pop music, and encouraged them to read and write about experiences relevant to themselves. The skill group concentrated on formal teaching, comprehension exercises and phonics. The research is summarised as follows:

Individual children in the skill sessions were troublesome, but on the whole the children worked steadily with interest and enthusiasm. At times they became bored and the reading schemes seemed confining, but on the whole the motivation remained because the child and the teacher could see the progression from one book to the next in the series. Both knew what they were meant to do next. As he moved from book to book of the series, the child believed he was progressing and the teacher believed she was keeping track of and helping progress; this led to mutual feelings of satisfaction, and increased effort. The same satisfaction came from phonic work, completion of comprehension exercises and so on. One teacher said: 'I'm certain I preferred the skill-centred approach because all concerned worked consistently very hard indeed. Each lesson, one felt satisfaction in the skill-centred group's achievement. The feeling was not always achieved with the interest-centred group, particularly in the latter stages, when interest was fading.' Skill sessions seemed to encourage reading outside lessons, as the children wanted to borrow books in order to get further through the reading scheme.

The children's more favourable reactions to skill sessions were reflected in results from tests and questionnaires given to the children and teachers. The skill group made significantly more progress than the interest group in improvement in reading ability: in the five months during which the sessions lasted, the skill group made 5.7 months' progress in terms of reading age, and the interest group made 4.2 months' progress . . .

The teachers' preferences between the two approaches changed during the course of the sessions. At the start, four teachers favoured interest sessions, four were neutral and only one preferred skill sessions. Interest sessions were preferred partly because they seemed to line up with contemporary thinking on education. However, by the end of the sessions, four teachers preferred skill sessions, five were neutral, and not one preferred interest sessions.

New Society, 5 February 1976.

Openness in Schools. An Evaluation Study, by Ross Traub, Joel Weiss, and Charles Fisher, with Donald Musella and Sar Khan, Ontario Institute for Studies in Education, 1976. This is a study of Roman Catholic schools in Ontario. A complex study was made of open and traditional schools, with careful analysis of different social areas. The conclusion reads: 'the results indicated no consistent trend in the relationships between cognitive achievement and openness of programme for students of suburban, middle-class backgrounds, while results favouring less open programmes over more open programmes were found for those students characterised as having inner-city backgrounds and parents speaking English as their second language.' They recommend that for these schools 'it may be desirable to implement some form of less open programme.'

This study came out with some findings *in favour of* informal schools. In the middle-class areas open schools reported more 'positive' attitudes from the children. The eleven-year-olds appeared to have more initiative and 'responsibility to self', though the authors speculate that these more positive attitudes may be a function of the newness of open schools. We are not surprised by this. The *Black Papers* have always stressed that informal teaching does have its place in school programmes, and that children in excessively formal schools may become too passive.

All these studies, particularly the small-scale ones, are easy to criticise. It is very difficult to set up a research project on formal and informal teaching. There are so many imponderables. How can the quality of individual teachers be assessed? How much instruction is being carried out at home by parents? It is not surprising that inconsistencies occur. When all this is said, these reports, of which the Bennett is the most important, consistently demonstrate the superiority of formal teaching in training children in basic subjects. There is now an accumulation of evidence that informal methods in the average classroom lower standards. This is what the *Black Papers* have been saying for the last eight years.

Decline in standards

The evidence of research is backed up by personal testimony. Patrick Moore's complaints in this *Black Paper* are echoed on all sides. Here are some examples:

> One comment often made on the unemployed school-leavers is that many of them are unemployable, because their education has not fitted them for employment. On 24 January you reported that 'Britain's leading professional bodies are likely to call for measures to improve literacy in schools', and on 19 August you quoted from an article in which the head of the Post Office appointments centre had expressed disquiet 'over the difficulties now being encountered with poor writing and numerical skills'. It would be lamentably easy to multiply similar complaints from a wide variety of potential employers.
>
> *Hugh Sykes Davies*, St John's College
> (*The Times*, 15 October 1975.)

> As managing director of an engineering company wishing to take on apprentices, I feel I must point out the experience of my personnel manager where school-leavers are concerned. Since the summer he has failed completely among many interviewed to find a single youngster with educational standards which might be considered suitable for the training available. The local training group has assisted in this task with similar results . . .
>
> To give some indication of why we turned down those who applied; *none was able to answer the following:*
> Express $\frac{1}{4}$ as a decimal.
> How do you multiply by 10 using decimals?
> Having been shown how to answer question 2—how do you divide by 10 using decimals?
>
> *D. J. E. Lewis*
> (*Financial Times*, 30 December 1975.)

There was concern, however, that some students in the sciences, technology and modern languages seemed to be entering universities without information and skills they should have learned at school. The committee was worried that if the trend continued it might mean that courses would have to be lengthened so that students could catch up.

Speaking in London this week, Sir Frederick Dainton, UGC chairman, said: 'Students are coming to university without the sheer skill to use mathematical equations. Their use of mathematical concepts is not as high as that which is regarded as necessary if they are going to be able to graduate in professional fields three years later. Universities are increasingly going to have to go into remedial work in these fields.

University Grants Committee, Annual Survey 1974–5,
(*The Times Higher Education Supplement*, 26 March 1976.)

There has been a marked decline in the standard of qualified school leavers, Professor David Sharp, Glasgow University chemistry department, told a two-day symposium on science education organised by the Royal Society of Edinburgh this week.

This decline had come at the same time as an emphasis in schools on non-selection, mixed-ability teaching and integrated science. Integrated science seemed to have been imposed on teachers by local authority Science advisers and HMIs.

The proposal of *Science, a Curriculum Model for the 1980s* (Occasional Paper No. 1) would further lower standards. He could not see why it should not be permissible to take three science subjects to O-grade.

The proposals to put pupils of all abilities into the core course was bad for both the least and most able. Those dealing with the next level of education would have to work on what had been learnt by the majority, and a lot more had to be learnt about modular courses before these should be accepted.

Professor David Sharp,
Department of Chemistry, Glasgow,
(*The Times Educational Supplement*, Scotland, 30 April 1976.)

Evidence that pupils transferring to secondary schools cannot do even simple calculations and of a mis-match between primary and secondary mathematics is contained in a report to the Berkshire Education Committee from their director of education, Mr John Hornsby.

Only 11 out of 52 secondary schools in the county were satisfied with children's arithmetic. Twenty-nine were concerned about the difficulties caused by children from a variety of primary schools, each doing different mathematics.

Forty-six per cent arrived at one school with 'no firm grounding in the basic principles of arithmetic' and 'only a hazy idea of simple number'. Two-thirds of the intake at another did not know their tables.

> Report of *Mr John Hornsby*
> to Berkshire Education Committee,
> (*The Times Educational Supplement*, 14 May 1976.)

Dame Evelyn Denington, a Labour Party leader in London for many years, ex-teacher and active promoter of comprehensive education, is far from convinced now about the way education has turned out:

> I think we need to go back and look at the ways in which we did turn out children who could read, who could add up, who could spell reasonably and write decently, and who were not, as some people suggest, dragooned or brow-beaten. They were happy.
>
> (*The Times Educational Supplement*, 23 May 1976.)

William Tyndale School

Our sympathies are with Mr Ellis but our main concern must be for the children in his school. He is an experienced and competent teacher seduced by the fashionable and naive theories of the progressive Establishment. The Auld Report sums up his innovations as follows:

> There would be no timetable, the children would be largely free to choose for themselves from a wide range of activities, including the basic skills, what they wanted to do, and the team teachers would move freely among the group giving attention and encouragement to small numbers of children and individual children as the need arose. It would also be the aim that each child should receive some tuition in the basic skills on a fairly regular basis, but the regularity and the method of approach would depend upon the team teachers' assessment of the child's willingness and ability to cope with such learning activity.

These are all accepted procedures in progressive education. The *Black Papers* have repeatedly stressed that such open programmes demand a very high level of ability and effort from the teachers. In the usual school they do not work. It was left to Peter Lund of the Education Department of the Polytechnic, Huddersfield (from his tone presumably of left-wing opinions) to point out that the progressive Establishment was responsible for the innovations proposed by Ellis and other teachers at William Tyndale: 'they were putting into practice some of the advice given by such popular reformers as Plowden, Halsey, Midwinter, Clegg, etc., so heavily protected by the walls of respectability that they were not able to come out and speak on behalf of actual working-class teachers' (*The Times Educational Supplement*, 13 August 1976).

In our view, the real enemies of education are the lecturers who have sent out and are still sending out so many young teachers indoctrinated by the Plowden philosophy. Here is Wendy Hawkin of Rickmansworth describing what happened during her three years divided between two colleges of education:

> The staff seem unwilling to reveal their own ideas or techniques, except to repeat the dictum 'Ask, don't tell'. No pupil, it seems, is ever wrong. Practising what they preach, tutors will accompany seminars prepared by students and discussed by students with gentle nods and grunts but never point out that anything said is wrong, rubbish or completely off the point. This leaves the student completely lacking in direction. 'Pedagogy' was actually inserted into lectures in order to raise a laugh, rather in the way a comic would use a four-letter word.
>
> In retrospect, one was expected to know already how to teach (obviously it had been covered by the 'helped with Guides/Scouts' on the application form). An art student would

probably even lack the experience of actually being taught his subject—might stifle creativity.

'Basic' courses in areas such as mathematics included a look at the impressive library of schemes/aids available, and maybe an assignment to assess them. We wondered sometimes how someone who had never taught reading could assess a reading scheme. Discipline was never mentioned.

Most things were learnt by trial and error on teaching practice, provided one had a patient class. (Can one practise a skill one does not yet have?) However, the most valuable times were during those couple of days 'observation' before the practice. In between writing frantic notes of names of pupils, textbooks, topics, etc. one might be lucky enough to be an informed observer of a good, experienced teacher in action.

Reform of teacher education is long overdue.

How many schools are as bad as William Tyndale? We have published reports on similar schools in previous *Black Papers*. Our postbag and the letters published from parents in the newspapers suggest there are many. An example was reported in the *Glasgow Herald*, 2 February 1976. The school managers of Wellington Farm List D school at Penicuik had clashed with the headmaster over his 'liberal' policies, and he had resigned. Sir Robert Scott, chairman of the managers, said that boys had been permitted to spend their time almost as they liked, getting up and going to bed when they chose, and opting to attend classes or courses of their choice and dropping out at will. There had been no regular programme of education, no restriction on smoking, vandalism had increased, and girls had been allowed to visit boys in their bedrooms.

Summerhill has much to answer for. But the main reason for the spread of progressive education in unthinking ways into State schools was the Plowden Report. We conclude with Professor Eysenck's excellent letter in *The Times* (1 May 1976), just after the publication of the Bennett Report:

How did it come about that so-called progressive methods were so warmly endorsed by the Plowden Committee when there was in fact no empirical evidence to support this endorsement, and when psychological knowledge was opposed to the recommendations? Why was it not until now that such empirical work has been undertaken, long after the damage was done? Why was it left to a private investigator, in one small sector of the country, to do work that should have been undertaken *prior to recommendations being made*, on a large scale, in all parts of the country, and by an official body?

Not to mince words, our children have been exposed to sub-optimal teaching methods because of biased testimony and amateur psychologising, in the absence of factual knowledge which alone should be allowed to dictate far-reaching changes in teaching practice. Even now 'progressives' still claim all sorts of beneficial effects of non-formal teaching without any empirical evidence for these claims whatever, while at the same time busily criticising the Bennett study for alleged weaknesses. Surely the rule should be that claims should never be made without good, solid experimental studies to back them up, particularly when these claims may lead to the abandonment of good and useful teaching practices, and the instigation of bad and possibly harmful ones.

It would be nice to think that we had learned our lesson, but it is difficult to be optimistic. Ideological thinking is not easily swayed by factual evidence; it is only too easy to change one's claims when disproof stares one in the face, and demand new and more extensive contrary evidence, *ad infinitum*, while refusing to back up one's own claims with equally good evidence.

In the face of ideological commitment, even the sad fate of the children exposed to these pseudo-psychological modern methods cuts no ice and even the suggestion that it may be the dull and anxious who suffer most is airily dismissed. The Plowden Committee and the Ministry of Education have much to answer for; let us hope that in the future recommendations of such far-reaching nature are better based on factual evidence, rather than on amateur psychology.

Conclusion

It is amazing that an age which spends such huge sums of money on education should be so completely non-rational in the organisation and methods of its educational system. Informal or so-called progressive education was introduced as an article of faith; those of us who from the beginning doubted its effectiveness were treated as non-believers deserving to be burnt for our scepticism.

Yet all the accumulating evidence indicates clearly that formal structured traditional teaching methods are superior to informal non-structured education. Is it of no importance to the pedlars of fashion that children in one year in non-structured classes will fall three to five months behind those taught in formal classes? In every other sphere of life such a discrepancy would bring an immediate change of method.

The question no longer is whether informal methods are less efficient but why they still continue in state schools, who introduced them and are our teachers still being trained in such ineffective methods?

The local authority and in some cases even Her Majesty's Inspectors of Education carry a considerable burden of guilt. As Mr Woodley brings out clearly in his article, it is the local inspectors and education officers who linked their names and fortunes with the new methods. They organised the courses, and promoted the attending staff. At a time of educational cuts it is arguable whether a *local* inspectorate is required at all; schools would probably be better without their continued pressure for change.

There are also many colleges of education and departments of education which trained and train teachers for a world of schools which does not exist. As argued by R. T. Allen, the first term (we prefer the full first year) of teacher training should be in schools supervised by a 'master classroom teacher'. This would ensure realistic training and would enhance the status of the classroom teacher. Two years could then be spent at a College of Education on academic subject courses separated, as recommended by the James Report, from training in techniques. Teachers must no longer be trained by ex- or non-teachers not in contact with children and the reality of schools. An inquiry is needed into how people like Mr Ellis of William Tyndale received their ideas and opinions.

Grants to organisations which have pushed disastrous informal methods must be cut and such bodies disbanded. Increased parental choice of school will ensure, as at William Tyndale, that ineffective 'progressive' schools are denuded of their pupils.

Finally, the standards achieved by all schools must be monitored by national examinations at 7, 11 and 14 or 15, and these must be published by schools (but with *no* names of individual children) so that parents, governors and the local education authorities can see which schools are successfully doing their jobs and which, at a time of a falling birth rate, should be closed.

THE EDITORS

From a disillusioned Liberal

RENEE SOSKIN

Of all the many words which in current usage have totally lost their meaning, 'reactionary' must surely rank among the most maligned. I am a teacher. I know that those who knew me during my twenty-five years on the staff of a 'progressive' school, as well as my colleagues in the Liberal

Party, for which I have worked during most of my adult life, three times a parliamentary candidate, as a spokesman on education for some years, and a County Councillor on an Education Committee, will wonder that I contribute to this publication. 'She has become a reactionary' they will say in horror. I totally refute this label. My life has been involved with children, not only through my profession (I now run my own school), but as a senior member of the London Juvenile Bench, and in bringing up six children of my own. As a result, one fact emerges patently and indisputably clear. Children are individuals; no single system of education will suit them all. The best we can hope for is to provide such a variety and such a diversity in education that every child will have the opportunity to fulfil his own potential to the utmost and to flee away from any suggestion of uniformity. I will not accept that this is reactionary.

Politicians cannot, of course, provide all the answers. Nor indeed can schools; they play only one role, albeit a very important one, in a child's development. That education should have become a political pawn is in itself abhorrent, with the two opposing forces more and more entrenched in their set, politically motivated positions. Could the Liberal Party do any better? Here is a Party which claims to be dedicated to individual liberty, individual responsibility, individual participation. Surely such a Party will consider the basic issues and problems? I have now discovered, with deep disappointment, that this is not to be. Where I would have thought that Liberals would place the highest priority on diversity and variety, Liberal Party policy promotes educational uniformity. Where I would have hoped that Liberals would encourage a system where parents, even of modest means, can spend money on their children's education if that is their choice, the Liberal leader has denounced this parental right; where Liberals should appreciate that the future prosperity and progress of the country in every possible field, including the political one, depends on developing and encouraging that precious and rare asset—good brains, I have heard a prominent Liberal MP say 'I am not interested in clever children, they can look after themselves'.

Where I would hope that Liberals would be 'radical' enough to take a fundamental look at one of the root causes of educational problems,

the colleges of education, all they suggest is that they become more and more like imitation universities, giving less and less professional training. What we really need is a proper training ground specifically for Infant and Junior teachers. These young people are often not suited to advanced academic learning but could make a splendid contribution in one of the most important sectors of the whole system, imparting the basic skills, if trained to do so. Finally, the Liberal Party has remained silent on one of the greatest stumbling blocks towards the achievement of good schools, the restrictive practice whereby an indifferent, lazy or even really bad teacher enjoys a total security of tenure. The whole battle should not be between one type of school and another, but about quality and excellence in all schools.

Looking at the field of secondary education, there is nothing sacred about an all-ability 'comprehensive' school. Given a suitable area, not allowing it to become too large and impersonal, with a highly efficient administrator as head, able to choose staff of widely varying skills and enough of them, it can be highly successful. But equally there is nothing 'reactionary' about encouraging academically orientated schools catering for clever children from all and any part of the community, which will stretch their abilities to the full, never allow them to become frustrated or bored, and which can employ teachers particularly gifted in this kind of work. Nor equally is there anything retrograde in providing schools which again, with the higher level of teaching and equipment, will offer a first class technically or vocationally biased education. These schools would make certain that children from any and all parts of the community will leave school literate, articulate, self-disciplined and above all, with a well-trained skill that they know is going to be in demand in the great big world which many of them cannot wait to enter, and in which they certainly do not wish to find themselves, as alas so frequently happens today—unemployable. To destroy what is good in education of any kind in the name of equality and egalitarianism is the most illiberal act I can think of.

The success or failure of education is in the hands of teachers, among whom there will always be good, bad and indifferent. All that government can do is to set guidelines and goals to make sure that teachers, parents and children know what they are striving for. The Government has a duty to protect children from becoming either pawns in the political game, or victims of educational experimentation. If we want to encourage wide diversity and variety in school planning and method, giving a head teacher as much liberty as possible within his own school, and thus providing parents with a real choice; it can only be done if there are safeguards, certainly until such time as the basic training of teachers has vastly improved. A national literacy and numeracy test for all children at eight years, and some form of carefully devised test at the end of primary education should not arouse the fury of 'progressives'. Tests would help teachers and parents to find out about a child's progress and take the necessary steps if all is not well.

This brings me back to what politicians and educational theorists often choose to ignore. What do parents want for their children? Again, of course, there are as many answers as parents, but from my experience of a wide range of parents that I have spoken to in school and in the court room, there are some common essentials. They certainly want their children to learn basic skills; they want them to be reasonably disciplined, which in today's world means learning about self-discipline, and they want them to acquire certain standards of acceptable behaviour. They want them also to have the opportunity and the teaching to reach the highest possible standard of which they are capable in any field of activity, and they certainly want the opportunity of a choice of school and a chance to change schools if they are not satisfied. Being a Liberal I believe that we should at least endeavour to meet parental requirements. So I will finish by getting away from sterile political dogma and back to the people who are doing the job in the classroom. The vital part of the educational system is in its base—so here are ten maxims, not original but often overlooked,

which I suggest, as a modest start, could be taught to teachers in training, possibly instead of some of the useless educational theory and jargon so prevalent today:

1 Children need to be taught early by those trained to do so. It is a myth that children will learn when they want to.
2 Children who work hard and learn thoroughly the basic skills are neither repressed nor unhappy—quite the contrary.
3 Classes must always be small enough for each child to receive individual attention.
4 Children work best in an atmosphere of reasonable calm and quiet.
5 Children need the security of a planned day, not a strict timetable, but a pattern and a framework.
6 Children respond to the demands of high standards in all fields of activity.
7 Children's natural creative ability is not in any way inhibited by being taught to read, write, spell and punctuate. On the contrary, their ability is enhanced by giving them the tools with which to use it.
8 Children of mixed abilities in the primary school can progress perfectly satisfactorily in one group if taught by a skilled teacher.
9 Children do not suffer by having goals of achievement to aim for nor by having their progress tested. Children with particular problems need more teaching, not less.
10 Children are all of varying ability. There is no such thing as equality and never will be; that is what life is about.

As a nation we cannot afford to provide eleven years of free education and find at the end that we have wasted even one iota of our most precious resource—the intelligence of our children—or have turned out into society one semi-literate or totally illiterate child.

Decline—and fall?

PATRICK MOORE

'I am a qualified teacher and I want to teach my class astrology, I would be very grateful if you would let me know what is best and if you have any wall charts, pictures ect which would be of help to them. In antisipation, Yours sincerely . . .'

This was a letter which arrived on my desk during the summer of 1975. It was by no means the first of its kind. Some months previously I had received a similar request, couched in brusque tones, from a teacher in the north-east, and on that occasion I had returned it, duly corrected in red ink and marked '2/10: Very Poor'. However, it was clear to me that the writer of the second letter meant well—even if she had no idea of the difference between astrology and astronomy. I referred her to some books, though whether she could manage to understand them is something upon which I would not care to pronounce.

At a recent meeting of a scientific Committee on Education, I drew criticism on my head by maintaining that I would not like to see astronomy, as a subject, taught in State schools. My reason was that it would inevitably be taught badly, and enthusiasm would be killed, whereas at the moment any boy or girl who feels inclined to take an interest in astronomy does so voluntarily. In any case, I hold the old-fashioned view that the first essential in a State school is to teach every pupil how to read and write. Other subjects should take second place.

Inevitably, I receive a great many letters from teenagers (and even pre-teenagers) as well as from teachers, and over the past twenty years a definite trend has emerged. In the mid-1950s, before the clammy influence of the child psychiatrists had reached its peak, the general standard of writing and expression was by no means poor. When I received a question through the post, I could understand just what the writer wanted to know, and I could therefore answer to the best of my ability. The situation today is very different. It is not only that the letters are badly written and unpunctuated; there is a lack of vocabulary—to say nothing of courtesy. I quote another typical example, dated May 1976: 'We are doing a school project on astronimy so I want you to write and tell me about it quickly.'

The writer was aged fifteen. I referred him to a book (not one of my own, I hasten to add!) and he then replied, saying that it was too 'dificult' for him to understand, even though that particular book had been very skilfully compiled, and had been aimed at readers of the 10 to 12 age-group.

Of course it is easy to take a few examples of this kind and generalise about them, but from being the exception they have now become the norm. Of course there are many letters, too, which are well-written and intelligently expressed; but almost all of these come from children who are attending schools in which the classes are kept down to a reasonable number, and where there is no impossible gap between the abilities of the pupils in the form.

In my opinion, the trouble lies mainly with vocabulary and in the teaching of written English. Children who come to see my observatory very often know a great deal, and in conversation this comes out; but committing it to paper presents problems which are often found to be insuperable. I must add that this applies to all topics, not only to science.

Nobody in their senses will deny that in State schools, the drop in English standards during the past fifteen years or so has been disastrous. Large classes do not help, because when faced with thirty or forty pupils in one form the teacher cannot give any individual attention; and the days when parents taught their children how to read and write before sending them to school are long past. Another handicap is the system according to which a pupil is placed in a form depending on age rather than on ability. Then there are the various crazy experiments, of which the worst is probably the Initial Teaching Alphabet; a child is taught how to spell wrongly, and is then expected to change over. No doubt some pupils brought up on this system end up as good readers and spellers, but I suggest that this is in spite of ITA, not because of it.

Listening to the views of modern teachers, one might imagine that it is a difficult matter to teach an average child how to read and write. Of course it is not, but there is no short cut. Until the fundamentals have been thoroughly mastered, it is only sensible to throw all so-called teaching aids out of the window, including television sets. Later on, such aids can come into their own.

What is not generally realised is that a lack of basic English is a hopeless handicap in all subjects, and that there is absolutely no substitute for proper teaching, laborious though it may seem. A similar lack of elementary common sense is to be found in other subjects also. Recently I was visited by a boy of fourteen who wanted to work out an elementary mathematical problem. It took me several minutes to discover that he did not know his tables; the authorities at his school frowned upon anything so archaic. I challenged him to learn them, and then come back. Two evenings later he reappeared, and solved the problem in five minutes.

Destructive criticism is all too easy, and I have no wish to be accused of it, so perhaps I may be allowed to make some positive suggestions:

1 Make the ability to read and write the first essential of schooling. If necessary, separate out the pupils who find extreme difficulty, and concentrate upon English as intensively as is possible.

2 Until basic English has been mastered, abandon all sophisticated aids, and return to normal teaching.

3 Ensure that all teachers have themselves the ability to read and write to a satisfactory standard. If they cannot do so, then provide special classes for them.

4 Maintain a reasonable standard of discipline, so that pupils who wish to work hard have the opportunity to do so. This may well mean separating the workers from the trouble-makers, which is only fair.

5 Make every attempt to provide smaller classes. This, of course, has been the crux of the matter for a long time, but today there are many unemployed teachers (even if many of them are virtually useless), and it is far better to have smaller classes in buildings which are warm and sanitary rather than huge classes in schools which are equipped with all manner of teaching aids.

It is a drastic programme; let us hope that common sense will eventually prevail. Until it does, British children have no hope of receiving the educational help to which they are fully entitled.

Decline in mathematics

ALFRED LEVY

During the past ten years staff shortages and instability have been a problem everywhere, but most critical in the cities, and few senior teachers have had energy enough to do more than keep going.

During this period, I have watched basic truths about the training and teaching of children stood on their heads one after the other with a wondering disbelief.

It is true, for example, that almost any teaching method can be effective in the hands of an experienced practitioner who has learned from the years how to cope with the tricky problems of organisation, recording and control, inherent in good teaching. These are at a taxing minimum even in the formal situation of one class in one room. They become greater with each move away from the traditional class organisation; group work is more difficult, individual work still more. Couple these with moves away from a set time-table, into options and choices (by little children!), and then on to such a thing as the 'integrated day' where there is no timetable and the teacher is supposed to ensure that each child does everything he should in each subject, each day, and you have an organisational problem that would daunt an unusually skilled and experienced teacher. It is totally unsurprising that such organisation has proved to be beyond the capabilities of the disproportionate number of inexperienced young teachers who until last year were passing through our primary schools. The turnover has been such (I recall one primary head who lost eight out of nine staff in one July) that it constituted a grave crisis unacknowledged by LEAs unless they actually ran out of bodies.

It used to be thought prudent to place young teachers under very firm guidance as to timetable and method until they found their feet, and so minimise the impact of a staff change on the children. Instead, throughout this period, experiment in method and subject content has been fostered by the inspectorate. Complaint about the inevitable slump in attainment is met either by denying that it is true, or conceding that it is true, but that it doesn't matter so long as the children are enjoying and understanding. To this I will return in a moment.

But there is worse, there are other losses. Children from this sort of atmosphere are only too often unused to making a personal effort as individuals. To be still, to listen, to concentrate, to memorise, to control their behaviour are all things they find difficult if not impossible to learn at the age of eleven. In mathematics, the obsession with the need for understanding before learning, usually citing poor Piaget as proof, is a major cause of low standards. I would take issue with anyone who set out to teach a process without making an honest attempt to achieve understanding but the implication that teaching the *use* of a process must wait until understanding has been achieved is dangerous nonsense which has bedevilled our children for far too long. They cannot afford the time to wait to understand everything; most are only in school until sixteen! Not only this, but every teacher worth his salt must have had the experience of teaching even intelligent children how and why a process worked, had the satisfaction of seeing it understood and then ruefully watched them devise their own short cuts for using it, such short cuts having nothing whatever to do with understanding. How many of us have introduced the idea of simple equations so very carefully as a balance of equal things—using a balance if necessary—only to find the children inventing for themselves the hoary but effective old rule, 'change the side, change the sign'.

But these are the children endowed with perception. The bulk of perfectly sound competent children are not so endowed. They are left waiting for understanding, and below the surface shell of cheerful classroom bustle, which is all the moderns ever seem to see, is a terrible awareness of failure. They are denied the sanity of an older approach which explained a process, taught its use, and required it to be learned, understood or not, in the knowledge that this would usually occur later and gradually. Mankind is fortunate that when the wheel was invented, it was permissible to use it without first understanding it.

Frequently one hears a low level of personal numeracy justified because of the increasing use of computers and calculators. But the citizen who comes to accept the work of these bits of machinery is relying not on them, but on the competence and accuracy of their operators. If we continue on these lines are we not heading for the nightmare society of a literate and numerate intelligentsia divorced from an ignorant proletariat? Equally frequently one finds the view that the acquisition of the basic skills is of secondary importance to children 'enjoying' their schooling. The implication here is that formal teaching is an unhappy monotonous experience, which is nonsense, and it is time it was squashed. If we go back far enough to the beginning of state education it may well have often been true, for classes were so large that many teachers had to be repressive, but not in modern times. I think the trouble here is that many people are trying to shape education on no more sound a base than personal, (and often imperfect), recollections of their own school days. 'I didn't like mental arithmetic so I want to protect children against it.' There is a lack of honesty, (or perception), about the nature of human beings young or old, in whom it is entirely natural to be lazy about the things they find difficult. Thus some people tend to accept their basic skills as being to their own sole credit, remembering nothing of the craftsmanship and patience of the teachers responsible, only the unwelcome pressure that made them learn.

Even if it were true that children in progressive schools are happier, the price they pay in under-achievement and future failure is much too high. While taking a fifth year group in the absence of a colleague not long ago, a large youth asked me: 'What's twelve tens, Sir?' In answer to my expression of horror (I'm a fair actor), he explained very carefully that his tables were in the back of his exercise book which was in his own teacher's room. Upon my jaw dropping a little further, a classmate supplied the requested information and ventured the opinion that: 'Yer ough a know'. To which the large youth responded a little huffily: 'You wouldn eiver if you'd a went to our primary school'—and the lesson continued.

Secondary maths concepts and processes, traditional or modern, stretch the mental capacities of most pupils, but given patient teaching, most can master them and even apply them in simple situations. The frustration and failure appear most often when some piece of simple arithmetic is required in order to produce a final answer. Multiplication facts which should be on easy call from the memory are obtained instead by a faulty climb through the relevant tables, or by a laborious process of repeated addition either on paper, or even with some children, many rows of strokes to be inaccurately counted up. Inadequate command of the basic processes of arithmetic results in calculations like 216×12 appearing as 216 written down twelve times to be added up! Then again, teaching techniques do seem to have become very faulty.

Children who are in an absolute muddle about multiplying a nought, or by a nought, or the necessity of putting a nought in the answer when division cannot take place, are to be found not only among those of limited ability, but in numbers throughout the ability range including the brightest.

Teaching a poor method, or teaching any method badly is one thing. Teaching false concepts is another thing again. What has happened is this. Teachers do not control the minimum educational standards required for entry into training; the government does. Over many years of teacher shortage, successive governments, lacking concern for either children or standards, have recruited students in excess of the natural supply by lowering the minimum entry qualifications. I read in the educational press that as many as 40 per cent of students have been admitted to training without the minimum achievement of O-level or equivalent in mathematics. Large numbers of such young teachers are now staffing our infant and junior schools. Insecure in this major discipline, they could yet have become competent in teaching basic arithmetic had they been given skilled instruction but most were not. It is these young teachers who find themselves under pressure to teach less arithmetic and more mathematics. To meet their need for guidance sets of mathematics books for infants and juniors have been written and they contain some surprising things.

This example, brought to my attention by a primary colleague, concerns a new way of teaching very young children to add and subtract. To begin with, its very setting out is seriously confusing. Instead of $2 + 3 = ?$ he is shown 2, $3 \overset{+}{\rightarrow} ?$ From this alone irreparable confusion is created between 2, 3 meaning $2 + 3$ and 23 meaning 2 tens and 3 units (twenty-three). Further, the children are supposed to 'count on'. Instead of putting say 3 shells and then a further 5 shells together, counting them and finding they make 8, the child, (relatively new to numbers), is supposed to find 3 on a 'counting strip' of figures and then count on a further 5. But while he is counting on 1-2-3-4-5 he is actually *pointing* to 4-5-6-7-8! How can this give a concrete idea to go with the correct symbol? In subtraction, say $10 - 6$ (10, $6 \rightarrow$), it is worse. The child finds 10 on the counting strip, and counts back 6. He is again saying one number while looking at a different one: another problem is whether his answer is the number he lands on or the one left showing? One asks, why was it thought necessary by anyone to alter the simple method of giving him 10 counters and asking him to take away 6?

Wrong answers spell failure in a child's mind even if the mathematical process is correct. How many adults, let alone children, will go on trying in the face of repeated failure? To state my point baldly, I believe that the causes of failure in mathematics lie overwhelmingly in the infant and junior schools, and that the downward trend can only be reversed by putting the children back to carefully structured daily work, to practice in each basic skill in arithmetic until it is mastered, and to the learning by heart of table facts and number bonds. And this will require many primary schools to re-introduce a detailed specific arithmetic syllabus.

Obviously some primary schools have resisted the disastrous pressures of recent years. I say obviously, because each year some children reach us who *have* been thoroughly grounded, who need only a little brief revision before beginning their secondary mathematics course and whose greater readiness for it and success at it are most marked. What of the rest?

Ten years or more back, I remember that in a rather under-subscribed secondary school the attainment of our intake, while not good, was such that with a concentrated attack on weaknesses, the majority could tackle the secondary course with reasonable success. In recent years in an always over-subscribed secondary school, the attainment of intakes drifted to the point where we thought it necessary to institute a crash course on basic arithmetic in the hope of averting later failure.

It may interest the reader, and it is certainly appropriate to look at a few specific results from the arithmetic test we use. Below are reproduced examples to illustrate the point. Beside each sum is the number of children out of 240 who got it wrong.

$$
\begin{array}{ll}
92 & 54 \\
-47 & \times\ 7 \\
\hline
\qquad (85) & \qquad (112)
\end{array}
$$

$$
\begin{array}{ll}
£13.24 & £16.32 \\
-\ \ 4.47\tfrac12 & \ \ 2.83\tfrac12 \\
& +\ 1.41\tfrac12 \\
\hline
\quad (232) & \\
\hline
& \qquad (196) \\
& \hline
\end{array}
$$

$$
\begin{array}{ll}
825 & £3.27\tfrac12 \\
-248 & \times\quad 4 \\
\hline
\quad (113) & \qquad (220)
\end{array}
$$

$$
5)£7.50 \quad (179) \qquad 6)102 \quad (168)
$$

It is worth pointing out that among those who could not work out these sums were numbers of children of good ability and, regrettably, it appears that outside arithmetic they have no knowledge of mathematical concepts that might be held to compensate. In addition to what is taught and how, is low expectation a part of the problem? After all, it's still true, isn't it, that we get from children in every direction the standard we are prepared to accept?

During my years in primary schools, and I taught in several, there was always a syllabus for each subject, for each year. How one covered it was left to one's professional judgement, but the targets were clear, and they were definitely geared to the standards required of the brightest children by the eleven-plus examination. It has gone now for good, or ill. What is there in its place? Many authorities are now using Mathematics Attainment tests produced by the National Foundation for Educational Research or very similar ones. Of its tests NFER says that they are designed to test the understanding of concepts rather than computation, and this is certainly true!

The ILEA produce their own and call them Comparability Tests and I took a close look at the two most recent. Without going into too much detail, the general picture is as follows:

Last year, 21 questions out of 50 required no arithmetic at all, (even including simple counting); this year 17 did not.

Last year the questions which tested ability to manipulate number, money and measures were at this level of difficulty:

$32 + 9$; $24—5$; £1.10—35p; 49×5; £3.55 + £6.80 + 45p; $618 \div 3$; $1.00 + .1 + .01$.

This year, the greatest test of a child's ability to add numbers is $4 + 6 + 7 + 8 + 4 + 5$. Division ventures into a three-digit dividend only once ($150 \div 5$); multiplication at its most difficult is 16×4. Command of money calculations is tested by finding four coins which make $62\frac{1}{2}$p; 70p—7p; £1.60 $\div$ 10; $\frac{1}{4}$lb @ 36p a lb + $\frac{1}{2}$lb @ 48p a lb; ($£36 \div 12$) $\times$ 5. One or two of these questions do test other kinds of understanding as well as mechanical ability, but why is the level of difficulty set so low?

Although fewer in number this year than last, there are still questions of a 'verbal reasoning' type which, by giving careful explanation of what is to be done, test nothing but a child's ability to follow them—certainly not any previously acquired knowledge. One wonders what is the point of them?

Allied to these are a substantial number of questions which could be given in simple words or figures, but are presented with the aid of pictures and diagrams. Why?

It was encouraging to find in this year's test one or two things the child was expected to know without an explanation being given, for example, the meaning of perimeter; but there were only a handful of questions, (I made it about nine), which would require an eleven-year-old of average ability to do some respectable degree of personal thinking.

Now this is the standard the Authority has set and it explains much about the present level of numeracy among secondary school intakes and their subsequent progress. If these tests are used only for comparing one primary school with another and achieving a balanced distribution of children to secondary schools, and have no other influence at all, I would still protest that this is a distressingly low standard to set to children of all abilities towards the end of their primary school experience. Whatever other reasons there may be for lack of success, their infant and junior school grounding is fundamental. Young children can absorb basic information, skills and habits happily and easily. By the time they are eleven even, similar learning is far more difficult and complicated by the changes due to increasing maturity. Why are we expecting so little when we can see the disastrous results on individual people and the dreadful loss to the nation of good ability

that is not developed to produce the next generation of teachers and users of mathematics?

Most of the answers lie outside the field of education altogether. Perhaps as a reaction to the evils of Hitler's Germany, the war and the bleak years of unemployment preceding it, the compassionate society was born. It produced the welfare state and a disposition to view criminals not as evil-doers, but as sick people in need only of help. The idea of punishment was questioned and the permissive society emerged. The schools are part of society and traditional ideas about reward for effort and punishment for idleness or misbehaviour also became suspect. This, reinforced by the powerful effect of Dr Spock's dicta (he recanted too late, didn't he?), by the media's interest in every innovation no matter how silly, gradually produced many parents and teachers who rated their emotional disinclination to punish children above their duty to do so. Now a sort of happy anarchy is of the very essence of childhood. Children have no standards other than those we give them. Without discipline they are as much deprived as if they were hungry or ragged. Without discipline standards of effort and achievement fell and thus new methods and subject content have been adopted that do not demand so much of the child.

Where does one lay most blame for the present situation? I think in fairness it must be placed at the doors of the most powerful people—the inspectors. Candidates for promotion are shortlisted for vacancies by inspectors and are appointed by managers or governors who have heard an inspector's views. It is no more creditable to teachers than to those in other walks of life that they tend to express agreement with the policies and views of such powerful people, although it is understandable. But these policies and views tend to lack balance. The chief reason is, I think, that part of an inspector's remit is to find out the best in current practice in the schools and to spread the good word. The problem is that there just hasn't been any startling development in the essentials of education for a very long time indeed. (Just about every method that is in question now has been tried before and abandoned as unsatisfactory.) Now there is a type of inspector or education officer who feels he must enhance his reputation by putting his name to something, and the search for something good has become a search for anything new. In thirty years in the classroom I have seen so many ideas pushed and then die of their own defects. Some were intrinsically good, but impractical, like programmed learning which required more books than schools could afford; some only worked efficiently for teachers of a particular type, like individualised learning systems. Some, like the Initial Teaching Alphabet (and here I do all honour to Sir James Pitman's sincerity), were fundamentally unsound in depending on teaching a child something he must later try to unlearn. One at least is permanent; I wonder who claimed the kudos for it? This is the open-plan primary school, a successful means of denying a child, among other things, the chance of learning in peace and quiet. I know one or two Heads who have done their best to build up the missing classroom walls with furniture, but it's no use, they can't get it up to the roof.

A teacher who decides he must challenge any current policy of the inspectorate faces a near-impossible task. I am a senior teacher in charge of mathematics in a large London comprehensive. Six or seven years ago, alarmed by the decline in numerical attainment of successive 11-year-old intakes, I spoke to the senior mathematics inspector about it. He replied that children knew so little mathematics when they left school anyway, he would far rather they enjoyed their primary work. Perhaps a year later I sent the same gentleman the deeply worrying results of a standard test given to an entire first-year intake. He replied that the test was inappropriate. About two years ago, having seen some sample results, the governors of my school wrote to the inspectorate expressing their concern. As a result, the new senior inspector and a colleague arrived, criticised heavily the amount of time my first year was spending on number work, and departed.

This year I decided to find out if I was alone in my anxiety and sent all fellow heads of mathematics departments in my district of London two questionnaires. One was to establish what degree of anxiety they felt about attainment, the other was to find if there was agreement on a list of vital numerical attainments for middle-ability 11-year-olds. My colleagues expressed overwhelming agreement (and this was repeated later, when I extended the survey to all of London), but at a sub-

sequent meeting held to discuss how best to approach the primary schools and reach agreement with them, a mathematics inspector condemned our list of 'vital' requirements with very few exceptions, informed us of the united opposition of the mathematics inspectorate and warned us of the danger of upsetting the primary schools. It says much for my colleagues, several of them much younger than I, that in spite of this they decided to continue.

Perhaps it would help to prevent inspectors from losing touch with children, if they did a great deal less organising of in-service training, (the value of much of which I feel is questionable, save as an aid to promotion), and spent a great deal more time visiting schools. Teachers should not be left struggling for long periods with intractable problems, say, of staffing supply or quality without ever a visit to see if they are coping or have sunk without trace. 'A problem shared . . .'

Authorities need to review their recruitment policies to give less weight to academic prowess or early attainment of headship and much more to achieving a balance of views within each discipline and in the inspectorate as a whole. Inspectors need to have wide experience of more than one type of school. It seems to me quite wrong to place a person in charge of advising on headships, assessing teachers and judging the needs of children in schools of a type of which he has no personal experience. I feel as strongly about this as about College of Education tutors who tell me they 'get to know' about the schools for which they are assessing the suitability of their students! To be fair, I have met some kindly and balanced inspectors over the years, but it would be pleasant to hear them speaking out against extreme policies occasionally. I wish it could be made obligatory for all who leave the schools for administrative work or teacher training to return to teaching children for a short spell at regular intervals. I am sure this alone would be a massive contribution to stability.

There is more that needs to be done. A child's education should be one continuous process, not two disjointed chunks, or, where he begins in a separate infants school, three. The dichotomy between stages of education must be ended. The inspectors could use some of the time saved from running some of those courses to set up in each convenient area permanent bodies of teachers concerned with teaching the two major disciplines—language and number. Inspectors must not attempt to dominate these bodies but to ensure that they do run well and smoothly and have someone of standing available to put their decisions into effect. And they would have to have the power to approve or reject educational developments in their area.

This would not be enough. Primary and secondary teachers may meet often, but the other's territory is still foreign. Primary teachers need to know the worries of their counterparts about qualifying their pupils for careers. Secondary teachers need to learn of the sheer skill and patience involved in starting children on language and number.

I would like to see a change in the staffing of schools with no teacher permitted to make a career in one field without having had a minimum period of experience in the other. Lastly, little as I relish any diminution of the freedom of British teachers to control their work, I do think we have reached the stage when minimum standards of attainment in language and arithmetic must be nationally set and tested. Although the damage already done is so obvious, I believe that the number of primary schools responsible for it is nationally still a minority, albeit a very large one. In the secondary schools the need of the pupils to qualify for careers is a much more immediate factor in the thinking of teachers. The reasons for falling standards in this field are more related to the size of schools. But there is already a small but significant number of teachers holding senior posts who say that the attitude of the children to the subject is more important than the number of processes learned. Unless we do set such standards, I fear we shall soon reach the point of educational no return.

In the beginning of state education, schools concerned themselves chiefly with teaching children facts and skills without too much concern for the child as a person. Concern for the child and teaching expertise grew gradually and reached a reasonable balance. In our day we have seen 'concern' for the child lose all proportion. The intention to do good has been elevated into a worthwhile end in itself and experiment has followed experiment with a thoughtlessness as to their effect upon the minds and futures of children that amounts to callousness.

By relegating the acquisition of knowledge to second place we have deprived a great mass of people and children of their right to a sound education. By a bitter irony, the most deprived of all are the children of those for whom state education was introduced, the children of people who are unable to buy an education, or to teach their children themselves.

The Bullock Report

STUART FROOME

I was surprised to read recently that a certain Director of Education had claimed in a speech to a gathering of teachers that the first chapters of the Bullock Report show that 'standards are not collapsing about our ears'. While I would agree with him that the initial chapter of the Report, 'Attitudes to the Teaching of English', does its best to allay readers' anxiety on the question of the alleged decline in written English in schools, the references made to the complaints of employers of half a century ago concerning the deficiencies of their newly recruited staff are so overdone that the discerning reader sees at once where the argument is leading, and is rather wary of drawing the wrong conclusion.

It is unfortunate that right from the start of the Report the impression is given that there have always been complaints about the low standards of English exhibited by school leavers, because interested readers, such as those who favour modern informal methods, are likely to rush to construe this suggestion as evidence that standards of writing are no worse than they have always been. It was a mistake, in my view, to begin the Report in this way, as it suggests to readers, intentionally or otherwise, that because people used to complain about school leavers' English fifty years ago, just as no doubt they groused about the vagaries of the weather, the duplicity of politicians and the weakness of the beer, things are not as bad as those *Black Paper* critics would have us believe. Before drawing this comforting conclusion however, it should be noted that while Messrs Vickers Ltd, Lever Bros, and Boots Pure Drug Co., whose complaints are quoted from the Newbolt Report of 1921, may have been concerned about the low attainment in English achieved by their new employees, standards of writing competence at that time were based on much more demanding criteria than those which are acceptable today. These companies were not likely to have been grumbling about spelling, handwriting, punctuation and sentence construction, because these fundamental features of written composition would have been zealously nurtured and safeguarded in all contemporary state schools, which were subject to periodic inspection to ensure the maintenance of reasonable standards in the basic subjects.

During the past forty years, as the 'progressive' philosophy of education adumbrated by John Dewey has gained ground in British and American schools, the teaching of English has probably been more adversely affected than any branch of the curriculum. The movement to an informal, easy-going type of schooling where teacher-direction, the pressures of competition, and strict adherence to a timetable and set syllabus of instruction would be largely eliminated, has had far-reaching effects on the way English is presented to children. Those foundations of good written English communication—neat and tidy handwriting encouraged in weekly lessons, accurate spelling through daily dictation, careful punctuation from a series of set exercises, and well-developed sentence-construction based on a sound knowledge of grammar, have been steadily eroded over the past three or four decades, mainly through the counsel of misguided school inspectors, who have ceased to inspect and have adopted the role of uncritical, genial advisers. Largely as a result of inspectorial suggestion, the cult of care-free creativity has had a large following, particularly among younger teachers, who have welcomed the notion that a rigorous marking of spelling, punctuation and other errors, as well as 'punitive' corrections, have a discouraging effect upon juvenile writers and stifle their creative talent. This is understandable; such a liberal course of action absolves teachers from the tedious and time-consuming chore of daily marking and correction.

The Bullock Report maintains that 'there is no convincing evidence available that standards of written and spoken English have fallen'. It is reluctant moreover to admit that 'creativity' has replaced 'formality' to any extent in British schools. As supporting evidence for this assertion it refers to the answers to the very extensive questionnaire sent out to schools and published in *The Survey*. These are certainly worthy of critical study. We learn in answer to the question, 'Is it the practice to give an assessment in writing of at least one piece of written work each week?' that 43 per cent of children aged nine receive this essential service from their teachers. We presume, therefore, that 57 per cent do not, surely a pretty high percentage, and even the 43 per cent who do must see a great deal of their work go unassessed. In answer to the question, 'Are some spelling errors marked each week?' we are pleased to learn that there is a 97 per cent affirmative response. Before assuming however, that this shows that the marking of written work in schools has not been neglected, as I claim it has, we should give a little thought to the implications of this response. What exactly does 'some' mean? If in answer to the query, 'have you cleaned *some* of your teeth today?' the reply came, 'Yes', we should not be convinced that the job had been done satisfactorily. Nor can any conscientious teacher be satisfied with partial marking of written English. It is a task for full commitment like cleaning teeth. It needs to be done wholly and completely or there is little point in doing it at all.

The Report also declares that the answers to the questionnaire prove that 'a good deal of time is allocated to formal practice in English', and they 'do not reveal a picture of the decay of such work in the midst of a climate of unchecked activity'. Here again it depends what is meant by 'a good deal of time'. We find that at the age of nine, 15 per cent of children spent no time at all on language usage (grammar, punctuation etc.); 50 per cent were occupied on it for up to 30 minutes per week, while only 32 per cent spent more time than this on formal language work. In my opinion, 30 minutes per week on this most vital factor of English learning is quite inadequate. In fact, if only 30 minutes of language study per week were given to a class of 30 pupils in a school where the modern idea of individualised learning was in vogue, each child could receive a maximum of only one minute of such attention weekly. This is certainly not enough. In a truly formal school, from 30 to 40 minutes per day on language usage and allied work would be the very minimum needed for ensuring satisfactory progress. It can be seen, therefore, that the answers to the questionnaire do not by any means support the claim that a 'good deal of time' is allocated to formal English work in schools at the age of nine. On the contrary I think they indicate a falling-short of the time necessary for effective teaching at this impressionable age.

Heads complained to the Committee about the poor standard of written expression of some of the young teachers who have joined their schools. I myself could have shown the Committee examples of deplorable written work by college of education students, including essays from twenty students which contained in total no less than 192 spelling errors, besides numerous punctuation and grammatical mistakes. On one occasion, when I did read to Committee members the percentages of students who had mis-spelt certain everyday words in a test set by their college English lecturer, e.g.: manoeuvre 85 per cent, embarrass 54 per cent, conscientious 64 per cent, supersede 83 per cent, and occurrence 71 per cent, one well-known lay member of the Committee said to me reprovingly,

'Jane Austen couldn't spell!' He might have added that Yeats could not spell, but neither Jane Austen nor Yeats were training to become teachers of English in our primary and secondary schools.

This Committee member's attitude to the obvious decline in spelling is in line with the lax, informal, easy-going approach which has been recommended by the inspectorate to the teachers of this country for many years. It is surprising therefore that in the Bullock Report there is no frank admission that there has been this movement in contemporary English teaching towards a style of children's writing that is free of the conventional restraints of accuracy which render written expression readable and comprehensible. Yet this notion of 'creative' writing, which it is claimed springs from the child's secret inner consciousness, and must therefore not be sullied by the teacher's corrective intervention, is quite widespread. Sometimes I have known the idea of the sanctity of a child's creative work carried to an absurd length, notably at a school open day, where children's uncorrected work was unashamedly on display, and two seven-year-olds strutted round the hall with their papier-maché model of a dragon to which was attached the proud message, 'We dun this'.

The Bullock Committee received some interesting evidence of this permissive attitude to children's writing in an account of English teaching in sixteen junior and primary schools in widely different areas, made by a team of Her Majesty's Inspectors.

While praising some schools for putting children's good work on exhibition, this report noted: 'In some cases work of very poor quality was displayed, with no attempt having been made to improve it. The motive for this appeared to be that the child's spontaneous effort was sacrosanct, and to ask him to improve it would stifle his creativity.' In a further reference to the growing addiction in schools to the concept of 'creativity', this inspectorial account of observed teaching practices warns against too impractical notions of what can be expected from little children who are learning how to write.

A laudable desire to foster 'creativity' goes along in many schools with the idea that children will develop the power to use language simply by being encouraged to speak and write but that any critical intervention will stem the flow. Observation suggests that some children develop hardly at all in competence by such methods, and few develop as quickly and efficiently as they could with the right sort of intervention and positive teaching of individuals, groups and classes. It needs to be realised that creativity in language is impossible without an accompanying critical activity.

I was glad that the Bullock Report reflected the sound advice contained in this statement, by averring that language growth cannot be taken for granted but needs the deliberate intervention of the teacher, but I do not agree with the conclusion that it is where the principles of modern primary education have been misinterpreted that this desirable intervention does not happen. On the contrary I would suggest that it is the relaxation of teacher-control, emphasis on pupil independence, and the utter condemnation of teacher-direction, implicit in modern progressive method, which have rendered deliberate intervention by teachers unacceptable to those who have interpreted modern primary educational theory in the way the originators intended. It is the true application of modern method which has led to the parlous state of writing in British schools.

Despite Bullock's assertion that there is no convincing evidence available proving that standards of written and spoken English have fallen, there is one piece of research by an eminent educationist which indicates that there has been a marked decline in the quality of children's writing in one important area. This research by the late Professor Sir Cyril Burt must have been well known to all members of the Bullock Committee, and yet it receives no mention in the Report, although there are four allusions to the work of this internationally esteemed psychologist in other contexts. Sir Cyril Burt was appointed as psychologist to the London County Council in 1913, and in this capacity he carried out surveys of educational attainment at regular intervals. He was also a pioneer in devising tests of attainment, Burt's Rearranged Word Reading Test being in common use in British schools today.

The standardised surveys of attainment carried out by Burt with London schoolchildren included not only reading, spelling and arithmetic tests, but also pieces of written expression, and Burt's conclusions on the results of his testing, which no educationist of repute has ever seriously challenged, make very sombre reading for those who are concerned with declining standards in the basic subjects.

It is evident that Burt's comparison of children's essays written in 1914 with those of 55 years later led him to believe that in the interval there had been a serious decline in accuracy of expression, obviously engendered by permissive teaching methods which seemed to him to ignore deliberately those ingredients of composition which render writing acceptable. It would have been understandable if the Bullock Committee had paid special attention to this testing by Burt of London children, and had respected his opinion sufficiently to incorporate it in the Report. The overlooking of Burt's findings is all the more remarkable when it is known that some corroborative support for his proof of the great decline in spelling between 1914 and 1965 was sent to the Committee by Mr D. Cookson, an educational psychologist with the Staffordshire County Council. Mr Cookson set himself the task of finding out if standards of spelling had deteriorated since 1920, when Burt collected the norms of the spelling test he published in *Mental and Scholastic Tests*. In 1969, Burt claimed that the median score in spelling of children aged 10 to 11 had dropped by 5.4 per cent between 1920 and 1965, but that there had been a more striking decline of 8.9 per cent between median scores obtained in 1914 and 1965. Mr Cookson, being unable readily to make use of London children as Burt had done, decided in 1971 to test Burt's claim by giving the 1920 test to Staffordshire secondary schoolchildren and comparing their scores with the original norms. 1,274 children in the first and third years of five separate secondary schools were given the Burt test of 100 words of increasing difficulty, (from 'a' and 'it' to 'embarrassing' and 'tyrannous'). Mr Cookson went to a great deal of trouble to ensure that the Staffordshire children were of similar intellectual capacity to the London children, who were of average intelligence and representative of the population in general.

The two main findings of this survey of Staffordshire children's spelling in 1971 compared with that of London children in 1920, are that first there has been a deterioration in the average level of spelling attainment in that period of 12 per cent for first-year children, and between 17 and 18 per cent for third-year pupils. Secondly, the standard deviations of the spelling test at the ages tested have increased since 1920. This latter finding suggests that there is a much wider spread of scores than in 1920, and it follows that in terms of test words done correctly, the worst spellers of today are further below the average level of today than the worst spellers fifty years ago were below the average level at that time.

It would appear therefore that Burt's disturbing findings concerning the decline of spelling competence by London children between 1914 and 1965 have been supported, as far as such a comparison is valid, by Mr Cookson in 1971.

Without the evidence of declining standards of spelling afforded by these two studies, there is abundant proof of the sorry state of written English in schools, shown in the numerous complaints about the slack, inaccurate and mis-spelt writing of many undergraduates and college of education entrants, who must be ranked intellectually among the top ten to fifteen per cent of the population. Bullock remarks on these complaints, but, surprisingly, fails to draw the obvious conclusion that if a considerable number of those in the very top range of intelligence are so deficient in writing skills, then the standard of those who do not aspire to be teachers or to enter a university must be correspondingly very low indeed.

It was because I thought that the Bullock Report had not made enough of the deficiencies of the schools in respect of children's written expression, and was clearly reluctant to attribute the deterioration which has taken place during the past three decades, to the adoption of free, unsystematic methods of teaching English, that I published a Note of Dissent to the Report. I believe the Committee of Inquiry had an unrivalled opportunity to state boldly and unequivocally that it was not satisfied with the way children's writing was being taught in schools, and that a return to more structured teaching procedures involving systematic training in the traditional accomplishments of spelling, punctuation and grammatical sentence construction, would equip and inspire our children to write stylishly, vividly and tellingly—or in modern educational parlance—creatively!

This was a great chance missed!

Who's for creativity?

R. G. A. SHERRATT

On the morning of Thursday, 30 August 1770, Charles Burney, Mus.D, went to a concert given by the Accademia Filarmonica of Bologna in the church of S. Giovanni in Monti. And 'who should I spy there but the celebrated little German Mozart who 3 or 4 years ago surprised everybody in London so much by his premature musical talents . . . The little man is grown a great deal but is still a little man . . . The Pope has knighted the little great wonder.' Mozart at fourteen, then, was surprising, and honoured by the Pope—but 'little . . . little . . . little . . . little': there is something avuncularly patronising about Dr Burney's reaction to the child prodigy.

Nor was he peculiar in this. One of his friends wrote to him from Salzburg about the young Mozart: 'he is one further instance of early fruit being more extraordinary than excellent'. Dr Burney's friend would surely have relished the expression, 'Little great wonder', presumably chosen deliberately in distinction from 'great little wonder', which is rather different.

As with Mozart, so with Schubert. Even with these musical early developers, we have to wait until their later adolescence before we thrill to anything great in absolute terms—'Gretchen am Spinnrade', say—as distinct from the 'surprising' and the 'premature' manifestations of a 'little great wonder'. As for a Haydn, a Verdi, or a Vaughan Williams, we remember little or nothing of theirs written before the age at which poor Schubert was dead. It is a matter, then, of creativity, using the word in any honest sense, beginning to show itself, in the most precocious cases, in the later teens, and in other cases, during the twenties, or even not until the thirties.

Every informed musician must be well aware of these facts. Every informed musician, therefore, could be playing a part in countering those disingenuous twentieth-century tendencies awareness of which led to the insertion of the expression, 'in any honest sense', in the last paragraph. The fact is that the educational world has long been faced with what L. Hudson (*Contrary Imaginations*, Methuen, 1966) called a 'creativity boom', or what Keith Swanwick (*The Time Educational Supplement*, 19 July 1974) termed a 'creativity syndrome'. I can remember first writhing at the sloppy use of the word creativity in the late nineteen-forties, and feel fully justified in saying that this boom/syndrome has been increasing for decades, is still increasing, and ought to be diminished. What possible virtue can there be in pretending that creativity, an attribute not possessed by towering geniuses until childhood is past, can and should be generated in the pupils of primary schools? What virtue, except that of demagogically appeasing the 'jealous society' (Reginald Maudling's mordant term, quoted in the first *Black Paper*) where 'enterprise and success are regarded with envy rather than with admiration', making it virtuous to concoct a fiction that all are, not indeed as good as your William Byrd, your Tintoretto, or your Thomas Mann, but better, being creative from the age of five!

The informed musician, in actuality, is in a particularly good position to suggest a more fruitful, a more honest, and a more useful concept. If he has thought about his art, it will have occurred to him that when, as a singer, he performs Purcell's 'Music for a while', or when, as a pianist, he aspires to Schubert's posthumous B flat sonata, or when, as a cellist, he plays Fauré's 'Élégie'—on any of these or a thousand and one occasions, he does not merely follow the set of instructions comprised by the score in front of him. He makes, or should make, a great effort of trained imagination, focused on the intention of the composer and the inner significance of the piece; by doing so, he hopes to get as near as possible to re-creating it.

Re-creation, that's the thing. But re-creation is surely also the apposite term for so many of the activities of that highly imitative being, the human child. Nor is there anything surprising about our finding ourselves using the same word for the executant musician tackling the sublimities of Purcell or Schubert, as for the group of children playing at being teacher and class, or at being doctor and patients.

But while the informed musician, we have shown, *could* be giving a lead in upholding a more truthful notion than that of creativity, does he in fact always do so? Not a bit of it! Take Dr John Paynter, director of a Schools Council music project operating over a period of five years. In his 'introduction to modern music in schools', *Hear and Now*, he tells the inquirer after modernity, 'music is about feeling'. Eric Sams (*Musical Times*, May 1975) suspects that the Paynter emphasis on emotional needs would make some readers feel he was more relevant to providing 'therapy for neurotic invalids than education for healthy children', and commands him: 'Find some sounds and try making music.' 'Instant creativity', as one less 'modern' college of education lecturer has characterised this approach. Dr Paynter is soon in the thick of it. He writes, 'Why not "creative music"? . . . you don't need first to acquire advanced technique: you can—indeed you must—just begin'.

And how *do* we begin? We draw a line to represent a 'space of time' [sic]. Then we listen for that amount of time and write down all the sounds we hear, say, paper rustling, a lawn-mower, birds, an aeroplane, a clock. Next, we arrange these sounds on our time-line—and, hurrah! now we are ready to be creative! We can imitate the sounds with the voice, and 'achieve some very interesting patterns' as we experiment with seeing 'how all the sounds can be extended in some way'. Very nice for a party game. But it is funny how children who have had the privilege of being taught like this and then transferred to a mere teacher of singing and staff notation like myself can express delight that at last they are getting something which they can recognise as music tuition.

After John Paynter, let us be further entertained by Albert Chatterley, known to many as a BBC Music Producer in connection with schools broadcasts. His 'Sticks and Stones' is a 'classroom project for young children and audience'. This purports to provide a non-specialist teacher with at least twenty-seven 'sessions' culminating in a performance before parents. In all that surely quite long series of music lessons, no time is found for getting children to use staff, or any other notation, nor for any systematic aural training: but (of course!) there is time for some attempts at 'creative work'.

So, after three sessions on a truly elevating song, 'O, what is your nose for?', the children are asked to bring substances for smelling; they then spend a lesson making boxes to contain the various odorous objects. In subsequent sessions, the children revert to singing, or to playing about with 'class instruments'—always, of course, by rote, or by improvisation, never via notation—then they have a session of finding interesting sounds to make from objects other than musical instruments. Two sessions later they are making instruments [sic] by, for example, putting ball-bearings in coffee tins. Later still, teacher tells four stories, leading to the children improvising with the sounds they have discovered. Thanks to these creative activities, the teacher 'will be amazed how much the children will learn about music as they go, providing you view the whole thing with an unbiased eye and don't expect recognisable rhythms and tunes'. Others may be amazed *if* these children learn anything about music, not *how much*.

Sad to relate, however, it has to be admitted that freedom from the creativity syndrome is no guarantee of soundness in the world of musical education. For an outstanding example, I have only to turn to the CSE music syllabus (WMEB) to which I must perforce refer for the benefit of young musicians who want to do certificate work, but are unable for any reason to do an O-level music course. The syllabus is all of ten pages long, but precisely one and a half sentences are concerned with anything the least bit creative. The half-sentence reads, 'and to set selected words to a simple melody of their own creation'. The other instruction is, 'Complete 4-bar melodies on the treble staff (no anacrusis) by inventing a 2-bar answering phrase to a 2-bar given phrase and by choosing a suitable answering phrase from a selection of possibilities'. Two bars! The candidate has barely got started before he must stop! And just in case he cannot do even this infinitesimal bit of 'creation', there is the second kind of melody-answer question where he chooses the most 'suitable' from a selection of possible answers.

No great obsession with creativity here, it would seem. But not for one moment need we suppose that this is in order to give the candidate more time to develop a substantial body of skills relating to the fundamental elements of musical ability. Consider harmony, for example. One does not need to be a very profound student of ethnomusicology to realise that one of the basic characteristics of Western music is its proclivity for attaching great importance and significance to the combining of simultaneous sounds and the sequence of such combinations, in contrast to the absence, or rudimentary nature, of such phenomena in exotic musics. Yet absolutely the only little fragment of harmonic skill called for in my CSE syllabus is that required by test 5(b)—the recognition of the three primary chords as they occur, in root position only, in an eight-chord sequence.

Another basic characteristic of Western music is its being literate. Great as may be one's pleasure at hearing a Persian folk singer, or an Indian sitar player, or a Japanese making stirring sounds on his bamboo flute, it is surely hardly necessary to admit to being a shameful racialist if one rejoices in a privilege which these do not have, that of being able to re-create, thanks to staff notation, the notions of great composers captured for all time by that notation. And how much skill in the use of staff notation is called for by my CSE syllabus? Take vocal sight-reading, a good test of a student's ability to hear in his mind's ear what he reads. In the practical part of the examination, only those who offer to sing, instead of playing an instrument, have to sing at sight, and this skill appears nowhere else in the syllabus. And the minority who sing instead of playing will be confronted with reading tests so easy that, in private practice, I should be disappointed by a child of ten who could not manage them.

The reverse of the sight-reading coin is presented by two dictation tests. In one, the candidate listens to a three-note melodicle and, given the first note, writes down the remaining two. 'Movement', says the relevant paragraph, 'will be step-

wise or within the tonic chord'. My pupils laugh at the insult to their intelligence represented by this requirement. Incidentally, although there are references in the syllabus to the treble staff, the bass staff is nowhere specifically mentioned.

What the syllabus is replete with, is an accumulation of requirements calling for little gobbets of information, as distinct from music skills: learning various performance instructions such as *p*, *f*, *cresc.*, *pizz.*, *allegro*; learning a further twenty-three terms relating to sundry categories of music such as recitative, *lied*, symphony, fugue, etc. Above all, the candidate has to make himself familiar with no less than eighteen prescribed works: a wonderful invitation to superficiality, not only because the number is so enormous (JMB require only six at O-level, and only one at A-level) but also because the CSE pupil has been asked to develop so little of the musical skill which he would need to study them adequately.

Faced with evidence of this sort, of an expectation in some quarters of a pathetically low musical attainment, it is not surprising that the most prestigious professional organisation for musicians has felt it important to issue a set of guidelines defining the minimum musical achievement which a child of eleven should have if he is to benefit adequately from the activities of his subsequent secondary school music department. Such a child, it is ironical to notice, will already have as much acquaintance with orchestral instruments and the different kinds of voices as would be required of him if, five or six years later, he took music as a CSE subject. As for singing at sight, one could imagine the guidelines being read as implying that the eleven-year-old should have a less rudimentary attainment than that exacted from those who sing for their CSE practical examiner.

The Music in Education Section of the Incorporated Society of Musicians, for it is they who have proposed these guidelines, consider 'that children should

1 have the ability to pitch notes accurately, sing in tune and show a keen sense of rhythm;
2 be able to recognise the appearance and sound of the principal orchestral instruments as well as the sound of various kinds of voice;
3 have developed an awareness of the character and moods of music;

4 be able to reproduce simple rhythmic patterns and sing simple melodies from notation and have a good repertoire of folk and traditional songs;
5 be able to notate their own creative work.

All very admirably and professionally ambitious—until we come to the sting in the tail. So endemic has the 'creativity syndrome' become that, at the moment of calling for standards which would constitute an inspiring and overdue revolution in the teaching of music, in slips that reference to creative work. True enough, the four words 'be able to notate' are transparently—and very worthily—meant as a knock-out blow for the nonsense implied by that instruction for organised chaos, 'find some sounds and try making music'. But was it necessary to mention creative work at all? The insidious influence of this fashion will be difficult to eradicate.

William Tyndale

DOLLY WALKER

Two and a half years after I first raised queries about this school's educational policy, the William Tyndale Report was published. In its quarter of a million words one would have expected all the vital aspects to be covered. It is disappointing, therefore, to find that while this curiously equivocal Report is long on what happened, it is extremely short on why it happened. Even allowing for the limitations of Robin Auld's brief, more pointers as to why would have been of value. When he does allow himself to expound on why, he tends to come up with the wrong answers, particularly where my part in this affair is concerned. This is, however, a very minor aspect. For all of us who are involved in education the larger reasons why this school disintegrated are vitally important to establish.

I believe there are three main reasons. First, the breach between parents and teachers which this case exemplifies in extreme form in the arrogant rejection of parental wishes by the teachers concerned; second, the intrusion of politics into education on a national scale which encouraged the rebel teachers at the William Tyndale School to view education in a political light and to subject education to their political ambitions; and third, the artificially created breach between 'progressive' and 'traditional' approaches to teaching which has steadily widened as a result of official support for the former, and unjustified stigmatisation of the latter as mere out-dated formalism no longer having any value for education.

These three aspects, carried to extremes, produced the William Tyndale confrontation which has at last disclosed the depths to which education has sunk. The salutary shock has sent tremors across the educational board, and promises to have further repercussions. At the same time there has been the inevitable gathering of forces in defence of the tarnished policies that led to the Tyndale debacle, as well as attempts to dismiss this as a regrettable but entirely exceptional case. While there were singular aspects to the Tyndale

affair, I venture to say that the debasement of education which it exemplifies is a reflection of a very widespread *malaise* within education in this country today. It is therefore all the more important to establish *why* it happened. In order to do so it is relevant to examine briefly the educational views of the rebel teachers, as interpreted within the school.

Broadly, they were that all children (and in particular 'deprived' children) have inalienable RIGHTS—to do as they like, to learn or not to learn; to decide for themselves what to do and where to go, no place being debarred *because* they are children (e.g. they were encouraged to use the school staff-room); to hold no deference to authority and indeed, to challenge it and to think for themselves. Every activity (or none) a child engaged in was viewed as contributing to its development and education as a 'social being', and hence was uncritically approved unless it was actually dangerous to life and limb. Teachers were seen as fulfilling their proper function when acting merely as childminders whose main concern should be to see that the children are 'happy'. The basic skills of literacy and numeracy were not considered of any importance unless a child actually *wanted* to acquire these skills.

It was a hotch-potch of ideas, none of them thought through, having vague connotations with Rousseau's concept of the child being allowed to develop 'naturally' at his own pace without undue influence. In other hands there might have been a grain of good somewhere in all this muddled thinking, but we have to look at the implementation of these ideas in this school.

At its most extreme this was seen in the fourth-year form under the 'guidance' of the system's main protagonist, where total free choice was introduced. With all restrictions removed these children indulged in 'crazes' for one sort of amusement or another (table tennis, using improvised equipment made from school tables and up-ended books as 'nets' was most popular). The teacher's sole gesture towards some educational content in the school day was to put up a list of activities to choose from if the children so wished. This list remained unchanged for the duration of the term. When two of his brightest girls actually chose to spend their time working through what he considered 'boring' English textbooks, he merely expressed his surprise at such a choice but did not take it as his cue to lead these two well-motivated girls on to more stimulating fields of writing.

To develop social awareness a class council was inaugurated. The tenor of discussions held by this body is exemplified in the demands made to the children's librarian of the local library who was invited to their class council to hear their views. These amounted to virtual demands that they be allowed (1) to eat in the library when choosing their books—sweets, chocolates, crisps, apples, anything they wanted to consume at the time; (2) to talk in the library without restriction; (3) to slide up and down on the library's slippery floors; (4) not to queue when giving in their books. The very charming Librarian spent one and a half hours patiently hearing their views, and pointing out that demands 1, 2 and 3 were contrary to the by-laws, while queueing at the book counter was necessary to allow other people to pass in the narrow passage. The children, however, persisted with their strident demands with such rudeness that she felt finally that she had been 'abused'.

Obscene language became the norm at the school and any criticism of this was viewed as 'unfair discrimination' against the children from 'working-class' homes who were only aping their parents. This was an insult to the working class, if ever I heard one, since it was the part-time duty staff, all of them local working-class mothers, who were most appalled at the language used by the children.

Educational activities by the children were not merely *not* encouraged but in some instances *dis*couraged by members of the staff. One young teacher who was designated to take a reading group within the school's vertically streamed reading scheme wrote on her blackboard, 'I hate reading groups' and sent the children to play on the adventure playground instead. These children included several who had formerly been in my remedial reading class who were very keen to improve their reading skill in preparation for transfer the

following term to their secondary schools. They came to tell me of this incident in some distress. The new anti-education attitude among the teachers confused and appalled them. The headmaster was highly amused at this incident and shrugged off my concern with a laugh.

In retrospect the headmaster's views are epitomised in comments made to me during the time I was at the school.

On literacy Why worry about it? Didn't I know that people built marvellous cathedrals in the Middle Ages when they could neither read nor write? Had I never heard of the scrap metal merchant who made large profits but could not write his name on a cheque?

On numeracy Asked by some fourth formers, who had been left in his care during their teacher's absence, if he would set them some sums on the blackboard, he replied: 'What good are sums to you?' He later justified this to me by saying that 'formal' maths teaching was now generally disapproved of. As 'proof' that it was useless he said that if I went into any betting shop I could see men who were *able* to work out their winnings at high speed *because* they *wanted* to know the results. Anyone who wanted to use maths would learn it for themselves.

On school work A worried mother who came to find out why her nine-year-old son was never given any work to do at school was told that her son ought to know that it was up to him to *ask* his teacher for work or he wouldn't be given any. To parents who were distressed because their children were truanting and running round the streets of Islington, he replied: 'What do you expect me to do? Make this school into a concentration camp to keep your children in?'

The effects of this so-called educational policy upon the children are described by Mr Auld in phrases taken almost verbatim from what he chooses to call my 'black paper', although it was, in fact, a 'green paper' for discussion at the meeting finally wrung out of the headmaster by angry parents in order to discuss his educational policy. Mr Auld reports: 'Instead of becoming "self-motivated" by the new atmosphere of freedom pervading the Junior School [the children] became bored and listless'. '[There was] a general *malaise* of aimlessness and boredom in the school. This aimlessness and boredom soon led to `bad behaviour on the part of many children'. '[Children] who had been keen readers and who had enjoyed going to school lost interest in reading and expressed a dislike of the new system'. 'A great body of evidence was put before the Inquiry detailing in the most graphic terms the serious deterioration in standards of behaviour and attitudes of large numbers of the Junior School children' . . . 'Children became rude and unmanageable'. All this was reflected in my 'black paper' which broadly embodied parents' views as well as my own, and it is significant that every item in this paper obtained the seal of approval of the Staff Inspector for Primary Schools when he was cross-examined on this document by my counsel, a feature of the Inquiry which Mr Auld does not disclose in his Report. Mr Auld's view of my 'black paper' is that it did 'untold harm' to the school, although he does not give proof of how he comes to this knowledge. An eminent psychologist (formerly Chief Educational Psychologist for Hampshire) with whom I discussed the Tyndale problems offered to testify to the Inquiry on my behalf had my counsel seen fit, and he gave it as his opinion that the school would eventually have deteriorated to a *Lord of the Flies* situation if matters had been allowed to develop unopposed. That opposition was engendered mainly by the parents' revolt at the meeting of 13 June 1974, which was prior to my 'black paper'.

It is significant that the Islington parents were not taken in by talk about the unimportance of literacy and numeracy as compared with the overriding right of their children to be 'happy', as though these ends were ever incompatible. They saw the school as a disaster for their children, whereas the teachers saw their policy as a success. According to the Auld Report, the headmaster, when confronted with 'the growing parental concern . . . refused to admit that there was any basis for complaint'. Yet these were not inexperienced teachers but well and fully qualified. Testimonials placed before the Inquiry speak of both the headmaster, Terry Ellis, and his chief assistant, Brian Haddow, as exceptionally competent teachers. It was not that they *could* not teach, but that they *would* not teach. Ellis's first act as headmaster was to close down the remedial reading department (which catered for the needs of almost 33 per cent of the children at the school)

to replace it with a vertically grouped reading scheme. When this totally collapsed without ever getting off the ground he showed no particular concern and took no steps to provide an effective alternative. Where in these circumstances can one draw the fine line between lack of responsibility and a deliberate anti-education policy? As one irate father astutely commented: 'What do they want to make of my child? Fodder?'

Here we are at the heart of the matter which the Auld Report assiduously evades, namely, the strong political motivation of these teachers whose educational thinking was entirely germane to their political thinking. Mr Auld's attempts to minimise this aspect cannot obscure the fact that a great deal of political discussion went on continuously in the staffroom, much of it behind closed doors. An openly expressed view was that educating children was secondary to the need to 'change society'. A quotation from Blake's *The Marriage of Heaven and Hell* with undoubted revolutionary connotations, presented to a class of ten- to eleven-year-old children (among whom were some exceptionally precocious, intelligent youngsters) could only have had one purpose. The form in which this appeared on the classroom wall was: 'Do a drawing to illustrate the slogan: The tigers of destruction are wiser than the horses of instruction'. Not only has the word *slogan* a political echo, but the substitution of the more powerful and familiar word 'destruction' for Blake's original word 'wrath' made it meaningful for the children. Remove the evocative tigers (these animals represented the forces of revolution in Blake's allegorical terminology) and horses, and we are left with a bald incitement to destroy rather than to learn. In the context of present-day social problems this seems a strange thought to put into the minds of impressionable young people.

Is it too fanciful to see that all that happened at the school reflects a highly successful policy *if the aim is to provide material for future revolution*? While the intelligent young must be indoctrinated to provide future leadership, the rest, deprived of the basic skills to ensure them a satisfactory place in society, will have such chips on their shoulders that a fair proportion of them will predictably become disrupters of society available to swell the revolutionary rank and file. It is difficult to believe that the instigators were originators of this educational policy. The close association of the reputedly left-wing dominated North London Teachers' Association, if not actual revolutionary organisations, is not without significance.

If these revelations appear staggering, it is because they have been masked by the gradual development of the progressive movement in education under the aegis of official policy towards ever more extreme forms, which have particular appeal for the younger and more immature teachers who eagerly embrace anything termed 'progressive'. It is a sad reflection that no professional body has been more affected by the current preoccupation with 'trendiness' than educationists, so that whatever was presented as 'advanced' or 'progressive' in education has been increasingly, uncritically accepted. The rebel teachers felt so secure on their trendy bandwagon that they were confident that they could outface angry parents, dissenting colleagues, critical managers and even the Authority itself.

In establishing the main reasons for the William Tyndale tragedy, it is with deliberation that I put the breach between parents and teachers first. Without it the lamentable situation could not have developed, but having developed, it was the parents who brought the matter to light. They called the bluff of the 'do-good' teachers who posed as bringers of 'happiness' to the deprived children of Islington, but in reality were making them doubly deprived by fastening on them the stigma of illiteracy. The Islington parents—the salt of the earth—were not buying that one. If Mr Auld believes that it needed my influence to open

their eyes, he should look at his evidence again. There he would see parent after courageous parent coming forward to give evidence who had never met me or even heard of me until the press reports brought up my name. The parent movement is the significant force that is emerging to shake the foundations of the bureaucratic education pyramid at its broad base. This is healthy, democratic and right, for to expect the education authority to measure up to the task of saving our tottering education system is to demand of the physician 'heal thyself'. If cannot be done. Parent power is needed to put us back on the rails again. A nation-wide Parent Teacher Association, to which both parents and teachers who are concerned about the debasement of education can appeal for help and protection against victimisation, is possibly what is most urgently needed today. Such an organisation would also further the demand for a trial of the Education Voucher scheme, which could be the eventual salvation of our children's education.

Whatever the aspirations for good the protagonists of the progressive education movement may cling to, this is now in grave danger of providing the soft underbelly where surely and insidiously the enemies of democracy can attack and destroy our democratic society. In the aftermath of the William Tyndale affair I believe it is vital to be aware of this danger, to reassess and review our educational policy from the Colleges of Education downwards, and to build a firm alliance between parents and teachers to ensure that our children will not be deprived of their democratic heritage.

A simple story

C. B. COX

Soon after *Black Paper 1975* was published it was suggested to us that we should write a feature on Waterloo County Junior school, Ashton-under-

Lyne, as an example of the best in traditional teaching. Mr Eric Beard had been headmaster for over 30 years, and was due to retire in the summer.

In 1976 Mr Beard became well known as the retired head in charge of the selection of grammar school entrants for Tameside.

About 85–90 per cent of the pupils at Waterloo are from working-class homes, and well over half are 'latch-key' children. The school building dates from 1914, with all classrooms substandard in size according to today's criteria. In addition to nine classrooms, there is a conventional hall, the extra classroom being used for remedial work. Originally an all-age, and from 1946 an infant and junior school, it was divided in 1960, and became a two-form entry junior with a total school roll of 300 plus.

Mr Beard's school was well-organised, with carefully structured programmes of work. The classes were streamed, with class positions sorted out twice a year and communicated in reports to the parents. The children sat in double desks and formal teaching was the norm. Discipline was excellent, with Mr Beard's cane in use about once a month, and only after a severe warning. There were traditional sports activities, with school teams achieving many successes. The school was divided into four houses, with the fourth year choosing their own captains, and there was an annual sports day with properly organised competitive events. In later years the school also held its own swimming gala in the school's pool.

Mr Beard was fortunate in not being deceived by the fashion of the 1950s which dictated that a child should not be taught to read until he is ready. He placed great emphasis on the formal teaching of reading, with much use of phonics and word building exercises. Each teacher was expected to listen to each child at least once a week. He himself heard every pupil read twice a year, in February and July, and tested them. Problems were discussed with class teachers. Children progressed through a series of graded 'readers', taken from at least three publishers' catalogues, carefully selected, and integrated, for the earlier years, with the Infant school scheme, with which there was always the closest possible cooperation. In addition there was a group reading scheme, parallel in grading with the main reading scheme so that at each level there were several group reading books. At least one period a week was devoted to group reading, the groups containing a maximum of four children one of whom acted as 'leader'.

Each class had its own library, built up over the years by an allocation of capitation allowance to the class teacher, to be spent as he or she thought best. There was also a school library, consisting mainly of reference and non-fiction books. There was a timetable allocation for each class for the use of this facility, but individual children could use it at unallocated times with the teacher's permission. The fourth 'book' source was the local branch library of the district, to which regular organised visits were made, as it is situated within 50 yards of the school.

Some readers may wonder why we are bothering to describe this school. Were there not hundreds of junior schools of this type in the 1930s and were there not others still remaining in the 1960s? We might answer first of all that there are many parents today who could weep at the thought that their children have been forced like guinea pigs into open experimental schools, and denied the security and high academic standards characteristic of Waterloo.

But our main reason is that Mr Beard kept records of his pupils' reading ages. The table overleaf gives details of all school leavers from 1960 to 1975. Of 1,236 children leaving the school during these years 1,111 achieved a reading age of at least 10 plus. Of these 1,111, 938 had reading ages equivalent to their chronological age or above. Of the remaining 125 only 9 failed to reach a reading age of 8 plus. These nine included children who probably should have been at an ESN school, but because of parental wishes remained at Waterloo. Mr Beard has figures broken down for boys and girls, but these are not statistically significant. Similar high standards were achieved in arithmetic and other subjects.

We urge that every primary school should keep records of this kind, and that they should be available to inspectors and governors. If Waterloo can reach these standards in a working-class area, why not all schools? Many informal schools do not keep records. When the children arrive at secondary school their achievements fall far below those of the pupils of Waterloo. These facts should be known to school governors and to the neighbourhood, so that action can be taken to improve standards.

Advocates of informal schooling argue that their children may fall behind in skills, but their attitude to learning is superior and more likely to produce good results at secondary school level. There is no evidence for this belief. A visitor to Waterloo found the children courteous, self-confident, lively and happy. Partly this is due to Mr Beard and his teachers. Mr Beard is a natural teacher, with an easy warmth to which children respond. But sensible order and loyalty have always been common characteristics in good traditional schools, in contrast to the indiscipline so prevalent today.

This type of school, with clearly defined aims, makes life simpler for inexperienced teachers, who can be fitted in more easily because they would be unlikely to have discipline problems. In an area with several schools, Waterloo always has waiting lists. Its popularity with parents is reflected in its amazing success in organising the building of a covered, heated, swimming pool. In 1963 Mr Beard set up a parent/teacher committee to raise money. The aim was £12,500, to be matched by a similar sum from the local authority. The parents worked with enthusiasm, and the total project was completed in 1973. Today the children have swimming for two periods a week, and for the last four years almost all school-leavers have been able to swim. Those who could not were mainly children who for medical reasons were unable to participate. The cooperation between parents and teachers is a sign of their trust in the school.

No school is perfect. In later years Mr Beard did not stream his first year. If he had continued for ten more years he might have introduced more informal teaching on certain afternoons. But if the result had been an obvious lowering of basic skills he would have seen this immediately from his records, and taken appropriate action.

Where do we go in the future? Towards more experiments like William Tyndale? Or to a system where all junior schools reflect the order, security and high standards of learning achieved by Mr Beard?

Waterloo County Junior School: Reading records

		Number of leavers	Reading age over 10 plus	Reading age at least two years above chronological age	Reading age at least two years behind chronological age
July	1960	70	64	20	4
	1961	75	69	11	3
	1962	103	101	22	1
	1963	63	56	17	6
	1964	74	72	19	2
	1965	75	59	11	12
	1966	76	63	9	8
	1967	81	69	8	2
	1968	78	67	12	9
	1969	76	66	8	6
	1970	80	70	13	8
	1971	76	65	10	6
	1972	81	78	16	1
	1973	76	71	17	3
	1974	74	65	9	6
	1975	78	76	14	1
	Totals	1,236	1,111	216	78

And madly teach— to teach

R. T. ALLEN

The crisis into which teacher training has been thrown, by both cuts in Government spending on education and the reduction in the number of teachers required, provides an opportunity for a radical rethinking of the whole business of the training of teachers. The James Report was supposed to have done just that, but one could argue that it was not sufficiently radical, and anyway its most important innovation—the merging of the teaching practice in school with the probationary year so as to give greater weight to actual teaching experience—has been quietly forgotten. I shall argue that the training of teachers should be primarily the task of the school.

1 The mistakes made in projecting the numbers of children likely to be in schools in any given year, and thus the number of teachers required to teach them, surely disproves any claim by central authority to be able to plan manpower. The result has been massive dislocation, cut upon cut in numbers of permitted admissions to teacher-training courses, closures of some colleges, forced amalgamations of others, students entering training three years ago with good prospects of getting jobs and now graduating with little chance of putting their long (and expensive) training to use. What a waste of human abilities and public funds! The rational way to determine numbers would be for individual education authorities, or individual schools or groups thereof, to recruit directly for the posts available in the immediate future—say, one year ahead, just as industry recruits only for its known requirements. Promiscuous entry into teacher-training courses may have been all right when there was a general and lasting shortage of teachers, but the disappointed hopes of those who have trained for unemployment as teachers should surely cause us radically to change the method of recruitment.

2 So far, students have entered teacher-training courses with no real test of their aptitude for school teaching. Contrast this with recruitment to agricultural colleges. Though students there are not recruited for specific jobs, nor have they been recruited for specific jobs and then sent there for training (as many firms send apprentices to engineering courses at universities), at least intending students are required to spend a year in practical farming before going to college, which both knocks any romantic ideas they may have out of their heads, and also ensures that they know what the lecturers are talking about. It is surely farcical to take on students for teaching on the basis of GCEs, school reports and interviews alone, to lecture them on teaching, and then, after two or two and a half years finally to discover if and how well they can teach. Consider the student who fails or does badly on teaching practice: he has wasted two or three years and, *crede experte*, it is far harder to make a career in one field when one has tried and been seen to be unsuccessful in another. Far better to provide the trainee teacher with a four weeks' course in basic teaching skills and then give him a term of firstly part-time and then full-time teaching to see if he really wants to teach, and whether he has the basic aptitude for this very demanding profession. Having successfully passed this practical test, the trainee teacher would then profit from theoretical courses since he would have a fund of practical experience by which to interpret the theory taught to him.

3 What one fundamentally learns in Colleges of Education and university education courses—that is, in those parts of the course actually given over to education—is how to write essays and talk about teaching, or, worst of all, how to compete for grades in a system of continuous assessment. The actual acquisition of teaching skills, the gaining of insight into children, and the development of appropriate attitudes come only in the periods

of teaching practice, and one does not undergo them in college or university but out in a school. It would seem logical to base the whole business in schools in the first place.

4 From my own observation over four years I find little positive correlation between proficiency at education theory—writing essays about education—and proficiency in the classroom. Several expert essay-writers prove to be only average or mediocre teachers. This raises a large question as to the purpose and value of education theory in the first place; most of the time spent in a college course is on theory, and comparatively little on actual teaching practice, some 14 weeks or so, plus some half-days.

5 Not only may we question the practical relevance of education theory but we can point to cases where it is definitely counter-productive. For example, some elements of sociology of education, as in *Knowledge and Control*, leave many students with the impression that schools are a middle-class conspiracy to force an alien culture upon the working classes. Again, an older generation received extreme progressive and child-centred theories which reduced the teacher to a passive onlooker while the child discovered everything for himself. The notion of 'reading readiness' suggested that it was a waste of time, if not definitely harmful, positively to teach children to read. It is important to note here the situation of the lecturer in a college of education or a university education department: *he does not have to live with the results of his doctrines*. If he is wrong, then it is his students who, if they practise what he preaches, will experience the failure and falseness of his ideas, while he himself remains immune to their disastrous consequences. Equally, there is a natural temptation for him to make a name for himself by propagating new ideas, ideas which may well not have had the test of practice. This happens in respect of curriculum subjects and methods, especially when, instead of giving his students sound grounding in basic classroom skills, he launches through them some innovation, often as yet untested, which requires advanced teaching competence and is more of an extra, a supplement, than a fundamental part of the teaching of the subject.

6 It has been assumed that the student in two or three years will receive a training sufficient for a life-time's teaching. True, there is a new emphasis on in-service training, but this has not led to a revision of the schemes of initial training. What is surely needed there is the development of basic competence: more advanced skills, curricula and ideas can surely be left to later, after the trainee teacher has finished his apprenticeship.

7 The present scheme of training either takes good teachers out of schools altogether, when they become college or university lecturers, or provides a haven for those who wish to escape school, so that either schools suffer immediately, in the former case, or the wrong sort of person ends up training teachers, in the second. If the trainers of teachers were themselves to continue as school-teachers, then the schools would not wholly lose their services and the right persons would do the training. Furthermore, the promotion structure gives very little reward for good school-teaching: one earns more by taking upon oneself other duties, as head of department or careers master or counsellor, and so on. A system of teacher-trainers would enable the expert school-teacher to gain promotion and reward for his classroom proficiency. Yet again, the college lecturer becomes isolated from the chalk-face, memories of which fade. It is no answer for lecturers to go back to school-teaching from time to time, since then they might continue to escape having to live with the consequences of their ideas, like Governments which go to the country soon after an inflationary budget.

These considerations suggest an entirely new scheme of training. Without insisting on precise details, I shall give below an outline of a possible alternative.

(a) Students would be recruited for teaching after attaining appropriate levels of general education and whatever specialised knowledge they may require. At present, colleges of education both teach more about a subject and also about how to teach it, whereas university PGCE courses are concerned only with the latter. Extended sixth-form courses, technical colleges and polytechnics, as well as universities, could provide the additional education and specialised knowledge required. Where a specialised subject knowledge is not required, as is probably the case with infants and juniors, then there would be no reason why students should not go straight into teacher-training (but see paragraph (j)). We need to recognise the need for different abilities in the different stages of education: specialised knowledge and skill become more important as the pupils grow older. Incidentally, proposals for making teaching an all-graduate profession will mean either the issuing of sub-standard degrees or the prevention of many suitable but not very academic people from entry to teaching—those very good at getting on with, communicating to and enthusing children, but not very good at writing essays. Many aspects of school-teaching, and not just infants and juniors, surely do not require a degree for their competent execution.

(b) Trainee teachers would be recruited for specific jobs by each school, group of schools or education authority, or private body, as in the case of Church schools.

(c) Each trainee would receive a salary, not a grant, which he would earn, and so would be ended the abuse of colleges of education by students (mostly female) who go there for three or four pleasant and not very demanding years with little intention of doing actual teaching after they leave. For the great amount of money put into teacher training, the public gets comparatively little in terms of actual numbers of years spent teaching after training.

(d) Each trainee would receive about four weeks' instruction in basic classroom methods and skills, so that he could make a competent start with some of the teacher's normal duties. He would not be expected to do everything from the start.

(e) He would then spend a term in actual teaching under the close supervision and guidance of a specially upgraded and financially rewarded teacher-trainer, who would gradually hand over to him more and more of his work and timetable, so that for the last few weeks he would, if at all competent, be teaching full time.

(f) All students would then be assessed as competent or incompetent, and could proceed further only if passed as competent. Those who find out that they are not suited for teaching would have spent only three months or so in doing this, and would not be handicapped in taking up other careers.

(g) After the initial term, trainees would be-come apprentice teachers, receive a rise in salary (the initial salary could be relatively low and the rise quite substantial), and then could continue either teaching part time, with day release for themselves *and* their teacher trainers, to attend local teachers' centres for whatever theory, mock-exercises, discussion, and so on would be held to be appropriate. A period could be spent in full-time study, but the former scheme would have the merit of continuing vital contact with the realities of schools and children.

(h) After completion of this second phase of training, say one to two years, apprentices would graduate as qualified teachers and move on to the full salary scale and teach without supervision as ordinary school-teachers.

(i) In the former alternative in (g), the local teachers' centres would be staffed basically by teacher-trainers, so as to avoid the evils of remoteness from concrete teaching in schools. Visiting experts could supplement the courses run by the teacher-trainers themselves. An incidental benefit of this scheme would be that expensive residential blocks, empty for twenty weeks in the year, would be unnecessary. Just like apprentices in industry, one would learn on the job and by day-release, and would thus not have to be accommodated away from home at vast expense.

(j) A final suggestion: opportunity could be taken to break the limiting school-college-school circuit by insisting on a year's full-time employment (not loafing around) in something quite different from teaching before one could start to train as a teacher. This would help many to grow up who at the moment do not, and would give valuable experience of the real world outside schools and colleges.

Colleagues have made several objections to such a scheme. Mostly they are in terms of distrust of the ability of school-teachers to be teacher-trainers, and of the restrictive experience offered by training in only one school. The former is but the academic's contempt for the hard-pressed practitioner. If school-teachers themselves are incompetent, then they are to blame who trained them, namely the very college lecturers who express contempt for them. As to the second, PGCE courses give experience of only one school, and Colleges of Education of two or three at the most. And one could write into the new scheme a requirement for transfer to another school in the second part of the programme.

Finally, the *tu quoque*, which I fully accept. Yes, I am a lecturer, a lecturer in education, and in the most abstract part of it—philosophy of education. I fully accept that what I have to offer is of no immediate benefit to new teachers, except in so far as I can undermine the underminers and restore confidence in common sense and discredit the ideologies of the doctrinaires. What I and others do is much more appropriate at a later stage, after teachers have mastered elementary techniques and when they take on, or are about to take on further responsibilities, as heads of department, deputy heads or heads. Once we accept that *initial* training is for *initial* teaching, then we shall cut it down as regards theory, extend it as regards practice and do it in the only place in which it can be done—the school. And we shall also recognise that more complex and more responsible levels of teaching will need training above and beyond that for basic teaching. This is where the more sophisticated and theoretical elements are likely to have a genuine function. The question is: What do we want to do—provide easy jobs for classroom refugees, and free finishing schools for lower-middle-class girls, or produce sound and competent school-teachers? If the latter, then we shall want something like what has been sketched above.

The American scene

A. Bartlett Giamatti

*A. Bartlett Giamatti
is Professor of English
and
Comparative Literature
at Yale*

Today's college students—the former grammar and high school students of the late 1960s and early 70s—have lost touch with the language. These were the children nobody remembered when The Movement was moving, when the rest of us were being liberated. These were the genuine young.

They are the products of the anti-structures of that time. They have come and are coming out of the 'open class-room', vertical grouping, modular buildings with 50 pupils to a room. They have come out of the 'new maths' and its concepts, its legos and blocks and set theory, not knowing how to multiply. They have come out of 'individualised instruction' and 'elective systems', not knowing how to listen to anyone else, not knowing how to take a direction.

They have come out of the sentimental 60s, where 'repressive' and 'arbitrary' grades were done away with, not able to take the pressure of grading. They have come out of a primary and secondary world where 'personal development' was said to be worth more than achievement, where 'creativity' was the highest goal and was often completely divorced from one of its essential components: discipline. And they are arriving in college often completely at a loss about how to cope with their work, with their time, with themselves.

But most of all, these present college students, and those now in junior high and high school, cannot handle the English language, particularly as it is written.

That this is so is no secret. The *New York Times* recently reported that, in the ten years since 1964, the verbal and maths scores on the scholastic achievement tests (SATs) have been steadily declining, and that the average test scores for 1975 high school graduates declined by 10 points on the verbal portion, and by 8 points on the maths portion since 1974. This was the largest single drop in the past 12 years. . . .

To deny language is finally to deny history, and that is what frightens me most about young people who can't write, particularly those who don't know it or don't care. They have been duped. By thinking that language can be denied, in order to achieve full access to feeling, they have of course become blocked and stunted and frustrated—and at the most important level. It is a sad irony. High school and college students have been encouraged to believe that language does not require work—that if they wait they will suddenly blossom and flower in verbal mastery; that if they transcribe what they feel about anything it will somehow turn into what they think.

Clearly, to have been told all these things—and millions of schoolchildren were and are told these things—is to have been lied to. It is also to have been robbed of the only thing that everyone *does* share, the only thing that connects us each to each. Language is the medium in which the race lives, it is what we have brought from our past, and it is what has brought us from the past—our link with who we were and who we want to be.

The moving finger writes
and having writ
leaves the reader to make sense of it

JACQUES BARZUN

The march of mind in education—I mean, its drunken romp—continues to entertain both the naive and the blasé. In the United States today, the new thought moves to the tune of 'Back to Basics'. The press and the expert join pious hands over the rediscovery of the simple teachables, what one of our least diffident educators terms the *sine qua 'na'* (phenomenon, phenomena). Encouraged by the latest drift (we have yet to see whether it is anything more), parents are agitating, demanding and obtaining 'alternative schools', to which they may send as to any other free school their fortunate offspring. For the alternative school is the ancestral school, where one is taught genuine subjects with the aid of discipline and reasonable, not paradoxical, arrangements.

So the open classroom is closing in again on the young: what an experiment! A superintendent in a large district has braved enlightened opinion and declared: 'I believe a child goes to school to learn something'—adding immediately, 'of course, socialisation is important too'. In New York, the reduction of teaching staffs forced upon the distraught city by insolvency has spurred principals to fresh ingenuity. A number of them have said in effect, 'Tell you what, we'll teach the three Rs!' Several states have legislated that the high school diploma correspond to some visible item of performance, such as eighth-grade reading, the diploma being given after the twelfth. All this is radical, avant-garde, innovative. I am waiting to hear the word 'breakthrough.' Galileo, Columbus, here we come!

No need to waste time enumerating the causes of this shameless reversal of scientific expertise and long public apathy. One of the most welcome influences, though, is the impatience of the so-called minority groups—Black, Puerto-Rican, Mexican-American—with the nullity of their schooling and their scorn for the patronising doctrine of the libertariáns that would preserve and cherish every deficiency of speech and knowledge as a precious part of the 'minority heritage'. 'Social promotion' has meant passing tó the next grade though failing in this one; the minorities want social promotion to mean what the words mean in real life. Their common sense tells them without argument that in order to take their place at last in the main stream of power, enjoyment, and respect, mastery of the rudiments is imperative.

At the same time, the teaching of one of these rudiments—writing—has been almost given up as a lost cause, not indeed by and for the deprived, but for the entire learning *and learned* population: the large numbers in primary and secondary school; the college and university contingent; and the liberal professions. Business employers complain, editors of scholarly journals add re-writers to the staff, publishers find 'brilliant' manuscripts in need of extensive elementary corrections, newspapers print incredible howlers, which are echoed or anticipated by public men—all this being at the 'upper' level and no longer mere jargon or inelegance, but steady malapropism and the blind-and-deaf syndrome that makes *benefactor* and *beneficiary*, *perspicuous* and *perspicacious*, *fortunate* and *fortuitous* interchangeable.

Not that insouciance prevails. Anxiety expresses itself in the rapid sale of books about rhetoric and style; but it is a question openly raised whether even the most eager are still able to help themselves with so refined an instrument as a book. In school and college the terminology for describing and discussing the difficulties of writing has been eliminated by the scientific linguists, who do not understand that pedagogy must be far less exact and much more stylised than science. In school also, the latterday reign of 'spontaneity' has bred a resistance to the idea of necessary conventions in discourse. 'Poems' and emancipated prose pieces satisfy the 'requirement'—which is obviously an entity not hard to please. But the resulting young mind is hard to persuade. It will argue that at this late date the 'rhetoric of Aristotle' (by which is meant a clear sentence) no longer holds and ought not to be imposed. This complacent modernism can only be dealt with one person at a time. Over the last twenty years I have in self-defence done precisely this type of handwork with those doctoral candidates who came to me with every talent but that of setting down their thoughts adequately.

The effort succeeds, but it is long and painful on both sides. Out of the experience, I have put together a short book, published last year and called *Simple & Direct*. Its chief claim to originality is its abandonment of the old categories, which have become infallibly narcotic, and its substitution of broad new ones—very few—to cover most present-day 'writing troubles': diction, linking, tone and tune, revision, etc. And the one repeated exhortation is: *think*, become self-conscious about every word, all the time, in speaking, listening, reading, even—if it can be managed—in dreaming.

Whether or not such advice can take effect on those trying to teach themselves, it is clearly not applicable to children in school. There, one learns from recent soundings taken at Chicago, it appears that one of the obstacles is the teachers' appalling ignorance of what good prose is. It seems that nearly all prefer the wordy and the abstract—the pretentious, in short—above the simple and direct, especially if a little awkwardness here and there mars an otherwise laudable lucidity. The so-called objective tests, in which one fills gaps in sentences with words chosen from a list, have encouraged this corrupt taste; for the listed words are 'intellectual' words, used there to enlarge the vocabulary. The sentences, moreover, are abnormally lumpy—to accommodate all the eight or ten words—and the entire exercise is inherently destructive of the mental activity appropriate to writing. I can testify that the half-dozen times I tried in good faith to fill those blanks my mind refused its office and I should have failed 'in writing', as did one of my students—one of the best natural writers I have ever encountered—when he took such a test for entrance to law school.

What then should the schools do, besides pitching the tests into the fire and telling themselves that the sailorman uses better English than the bureaucrat? It may give the measure of the failure of nerve that has overtaken the best of us if I say that when this very question was discussed by a group of which I was a member—a group characterised collectively by previous courage and wisdom on such matters, and distinguished individually by high achievement in various fields—the committee decided to recommend nothing before surveying the literature and consulting some experts who might have new ideas. The question posed, it must be noted, was not: How can we go about changing the situation, the methods, and so on, but merely: What ought we to recommend as fundamental principles, as genuine Back to Basics?

And after this negativism of despair, a second gathering was divided and disinclined to act on a modest proposal that had been placed before it in the interval. For what they may be worth, the heads of that proposal follow:

1 Spontaneity, free inspiration, self-expression are qualities much to be desired; but they do not survive lack of technique.

2 Good writing presupposes frequent writing, the actual practice of it, not mere recognition of what may be 'right' by filling in slots.

3 Good writing presupposes reading good prose, continually, as well as reading aloud and speaking extempore under teacher supervision and class criticism.

4 Good writing cannot be taught directly; the pupil teaches himself, under prodding and encouragement from a teacher who knows what good prose is. This awareness must include a sense of what themes and what degree of mastery are appropriate at each stage of mental development: some faults are more grievous than others, some merits more praiseworthy; and individual talents vary as to what they can best produce.

5 The training of teachers must match that of the schoolchildren: what do teachers read and how do they write? Who coaches and corrects their writing, and how?

6 The textbooks and workbooks used in school and in teachers' colleges are due for re-examination in the light of the preceding criteria; they must show the same qualities as are desired in the final product, the high school graduate.

At a time when most observers would concede that every one of these suggestions remains Utopian, parents and others who think writing improvable may be glad to know that plenty of foundation money is going into such things as finding out how infants 'organise their experience', which has led to the discovery that 'ball, dog, and car' are to them the most important 'concepts' because they move. I am enchanted too by these startling facts, but I am even keener to know how and when the *dis*organisation of their categories and the mature inarticulateness comes about. Meanwhile also, the College Entrance Examination Board, ever sensitive to contemporary feeling, is discussing yet again the use of an essay question in its examinations. The next imperative need will be to find, with foundation grants and preliminary tests, the one high school graduate each year who can write the essay.

INFORMAL EDUCATION

Questions

1 If, as progressives claim, informal methods are raising standards, why not publish details of the reading ages of children in all schools so that parents can see the proof?
2 How many schools as bad as William Tyndale are there in Britain?
3 From what source did Mr Ellis, the headmaster, derive his ideas? Where are his instructors now?
4 If children are assessed by their teachers rather than by public examinations, how will favouritism be avoided? If there are no public examinations how will employers and parents gain accurate information about standards in schools?
5 In traditional education teacher direction is overt, in informal schools covert. Which is the more honest and natural relation between adult and child?
6 Recent research demonstrates that children in informal schools do less well in basic subjects. Does this not substantiate the *Black Paper* claim that informal methods lower standards?
7 How will students teach children to read if they themselves have never been taught to *teach* reading? How will a teacher maintain high standards of written English if he has never been taught to write clearly or to recognise good prose?
8 Why do some colleges of education give no advice on how to keep discipline in the classroom?
9 Should not all people who train teachers give demonstration lessons?
10 Is there any evidence that the extension of the old two-year training course for teachers to three years and the introduction of the B.Ed. has improved the quality of entrants to the profession?

2
Comprehensive schools

75 per cent of secondary school children were in non-selective schools and at the same time there was widespread anxiety both about the standards of education in secondary schools generally and also about the standards of discipline. Therefore it was of the greatest public importance to discover whether there were any reasons which were due not to non-selection particularly but to size in particular, and methods of teaching in these large schools.

Quite recently a review was made of secondary teaching in Haringey which went comprehensive in 1967. It revealed a drop of 22 per cent in O-level passes and a 35 per cent drop in A-level passes in the past five years.

We are now embarking on a Bill which is going to cause a rapid change in the structure of secondary schools in respect of some 20 to 25 per cent of all the children. Ought we to do it when there is such uncertainty about methods of organising a non-selective school? If I was minister I would not look at it. I would simply say that unless I knew what I was doing I would not go forward with it.

Peers must not be put off if the department said they were making a departmental inquiry.

You cannot trust that great department any longer. They will select the schools in any inquiry. They will select them for the purpose of the inquiry.

They should not trust the department unless the selection of the schools was done by an outside body and the inspection of their results was done by an outside body. They could not be trusted any more.

It is a very sad thing for an ex-Minister of Education to say but you cannot trust that department not to be biased.

VISCOUNT ECCLES in the House of Lords
7 October 1976

Background

Egalitarianism encourages the lazy and the passive at the expense of the dedicated and the diligent.

DUBCEK,
Czechoslovak Communist Manifesto, 1968

The arguments about comprehensive schools have completely changed since the first *Black Paper* was published in 1969. At that time the bible for the comprehensive lobby was Professor Robin Pedley's *The Comprehensive School*, which claimed that the introduction of comprehensive schooling was raising academic standards for all children. On 6 May 1969, Mr Short was reported in *The Times* as saying that 'if he believed that the more able child would suffer in the comprehensive school, he would oppose reorganisation.'

Today it is usual to hear apologists for comprehensive schools admitting that able children cannot receive the same special attention as in grammar schools, but this is supposedly balanced by improvement in the average children. Mr Alan Barnes, headmaster of Ruffwood Comprehensive School, Liverpool, has asked universities to make special concessions to children from comprehensives. Where applicants are normally expected to achieve three A-levels at grade C for admission to a university course, students from comprehensives in poor areas should be admitted with three grade Ds. He pointed out that for some heads and teachers 'the comprehensive school embodies an educational philosophy which is egalitarian rather than élitist: the assumptions about the special rights of the able, which fitted naturally into a selective system, will not go unchallenged' (*The Times Educational Supplement*, 23 July 1976). In a speech at Manchester, he said that academically able children at big comprehensives could not hope to receive the same attention as at grammar schools: 'It is silly to suppose that one can do infinite things with finite resources. In the past, priority was given to the clever child. The philosophy of comprehensive education places equal education emphasis on all children' (*Sunday Telegraph*, 4 April 1976). If in the 1960s pro-comprehensive teachers had made such statements

their campaign would not have so easily persuaded the politicians.

The *Black Papers* have always maintained that the comprehensive school may be the right solution in some areas but that in urban communities a fully comprehensive system does not work. Today the problems are plain for all to see. In the second *Black Paper* we quoted J. W. B. Douglas's *All Our Future* (1968): 'It is however by no means certain that the able manual working-class pupils are more favourably placed in comprehensive schools . . . pupils of high ability leave comprehensive schools at an earlier age than those of similar ability in other maintained schools . . .' Mr Barnes confirms that this is happening, particularly from schools for ages 11–16 in working-class areas. Dr Douglas asked for more research, but instead we have proceeded rapidly with a variety of ill-prepared reorganisation schemes. Worse is yet to come. In his Manchester speech, Mr Barnes said that at present comprehensives are under great pressure to maintain high academic standards so that the system will be justified. When all State schools are comprehensive, this pressure will relax, and inevitably there will be further decline.

The comprehensive system is not achieving the goals desired by its Utopian supporters. Not only are able working-class children held back, but the new schools are socially divisive. They vary enormously in quality. Some are excellent, with first-class staff and facilities. In contrast, poor neighbourhoods usually have poor schools, and concerned parents move out. The schools and the neighbourhood deteriorate even further. We have put forward this argument again and again. There is no answer. The Labour Party prefers dreams to reality, and in the process the children suffer.

Many Labour supporters acknowledge these facts, and it is tragic that the Labour Party has turned this into a political issue. In our last *Black Paper*, Iris Murdoch, novelist, philosopher and socialist, argued in favour of selection:

Those who are upset by the educational programme of the left are sometimes told: don't worry, able children will get their education somehow all the same. This may be true of middle-class able children with moderately bookish homes and educationally ambitious parents behind them. Selection must and will take place in education and those who banish rational methods of selection are simply favouring irrational and accidental ones. The children who will be lost for ever are the poor clever children with an illiterate background who on the 'chance' system are being denied the *right* to a strict academic education which can only be achieved on the basis of some sort of selection. Why should socialist policy, of all things, be so grossly unjust to the underprivileged clever child, avid to learn, able to learn, and under non-selective education likely to pass in relaxed idle boredom those precious years when strenuous learning is a joy and when the whole intellectual and moral future of the human being is at stake? It is most surprising that a Labour government should be indifferent to the fate of this very important group in our community. The denial of rigorous education to working-class children will in the long run militate against the very social mixing which is supposed to be the object of the exercise, if it turns out in the future that our only cultivated citizens are middle-class. Not least of the dangers of such a situation is the possibility that learning itself may come to be regarded as a 'middle-class value', repugnant to those who hold 'proletarian values'. It would be hard to exaggerate the brutalising effect of such a development.

More recently, Alan Watkins, a left-winger, attacked the Conservatives on education, praised the idea of comprehensives, but then, in a bemused way, asked himself why the system was not working:

Yet the supporters of comprehensive education are now on the defensive. What has gone wrong? The simple answer, the answer commonly given, is that the schools themselves have failed to fulfil expectations.

The real answer is different. The administrators, the teachers, the sociologists, the psychologists, the education correspondents have, over the past decade, betrayed the ideals of working-class education. They have given the match to the Rhodes Boysons even before the game had begun.

We hear the word 'elitism' much used by such as Mr Peter Wilby in the *New Statesman*. His arguments, and those of others like him, are really no different from those of Dr Verwoerd about the education of the Bantus [also taken from the *New Statesman*]: 'The Bantu teacher must be integrated as an active agent in the process of the development of the Bantu community. He must learn not to feel above his community. He becomes frustrated and rebellious when this does not take place, and he tries to make his community dissatisfied because of such misdirected ambitions which are alien to his people.'

Yet all education is bound to be elitist, not because some people are better at examinations than others (though they are), but because some things are better than others. Some things are truer than others. A few things, even, are true, and others false. Sociologists or educationists—the two categories often overlap—who compare the Cup Final to the 'Messiah' are, in a transparent attempt to flatter their assumed audience, doing an equal disservice to soccer and to music.

I once knew a miner, Tom Thomas, now dead, who would talk to me for hours about Hegel ('Eagle', he called him). Was he being elitist? Was Aneurin Bevan elitist when he spent hours in the Tredegar public library? Crossman and Tawney did not think they were elitist when they taught history and philosophy to working men.

It is time to get away from the terrifying inverted snobbery of the sociologists, the education correspondents and some of the teachers, many of whom are little better than criminals against the working classes of this country. It is time to restore the real educational ideals of the Labour Movement, which can be done better in a comprehensive school—under proper management—than anywhere else.

Observer, 8 August 1976

That egalitarianism is a betrayal of working-class education has been a repeated theme in the *Black Papers*. Watkins's assumption that only Conservatives oppose comprehensives provoked a sharp reply from another Labour Party supporter, Mrs Jacquetta Priestley:

The most foolish of the assumptions is that opposition to a hasty, underfinanced and autocratic imposition of comprehensive schools upon our country follows party lines. This may be too nearly true in political circles, but it most certainly is not among the rest of us. I know that a very large number of old Labour Party supporters like myself have felt obliged to resist acts of doctrinaire compulsion that we believe must do immense harm in the future.

Perhaps the older among us were sceptical from the first, convinced that big is often bad, that learning demands an academic atmosphere, that there cannot be enough first-class teachers for everybody and that their numbers will diminish if they have to struggle with mixed ability teaching in a non-academic atmosphere. If so, we have had our fears confirmed by young parents who, to their pained surprise, have found teaching or conditions so poor that they have had to remove their children from comprehensives. More telling still has been the change of heart of university teachers of leftish sympathies who have to deal with the end-products of the system. . . . No mention is made of the fact that the comprehensive policy involves the destruction of excellent schools that have grown up to meet an unchanging need for conditions appropriate for learning and enjoyment of the arts. Perhaps Mr Watkins has not had personal experience of this form of murder. I have: here at Stratford-on-Avon. When I learnt that against the wishes of all concerned our quite excellent small grammar school could be snuffed out by orders from on high I felt a shock of disinterested outrage such as I have seldom known. It still staggers me that this could be done by a Labour Government.

In discussion about education the inadequacies of comprehensives are increasingly taken for granted. In June 1976, Mr A. Taylor of Sunderland was writing a series of letters to *The Times Educational Supplement* and the *Sunderland Echo* to complain that his son at Monkwearmouth Comprehensive School was being offered a restricted range of O-level courses: 'it is impossible to take three full sciences to O-level, so there is no basis for three A-levels. This is, in effect, a bar to medicine and other professions and curtails opportunities in sciences.' This situation was also described by Verity Smith, a lecturer, in the *Observer*, 29 August 1976:

Before the comprehensive system arrived, those who favoured it maintained that one of its advantages would be that a greater range of subjects could be taught under the one—much larger—comprehensive roof. In practice this has not turned out to be the case. Timetable clashes can make it impossible for pupils to select the subjects of their choice and hard times have led to some of the less popular subjects either being dropped outright or their teaching limited to crash-courses at the post O-level stage.

This pattern of omission or limitation is particularly noticeable in the sphere of foreign languages. The first to bite the dust were Latin and Greek. It could be argued that the classics had enjoyed a very long run for their money; that subjects such as economics and sociology might well appear more relevant and stimulating to young people today—as well as a less arduous proposition.

Now in the front line of fire are the so-called 'minority' modern languages: German, Italian, Russian and Spanish.

That many comprehensive school children cannot be expected to equal the achievements of pupils in grammar or independent schools is taken for granted in universities. Carol Clark of Balliol College replied as follows to Professor Peston's suggestion that universities should allocate a quota of places to comprehensive schools:

. . . it is my clear impression that at Oxford and in my subject at least, college tutors operate a positive bias in favour of candidates from comprehensive schools. That is to say, when they think they see promise in a candidate they are often willing to overlook some indifferent papers on the grounds that the pupil may have been less well, and will certainly have been less intensively, taught than a candidate from an independent school.

In my view, this bias is justified at present,

for while, as Professor Peston says, it would be unreasonable to argue that academic education cannot be provided at any comprehensive school, it seems clear that it is not being provided at some (perhaps many) such schools today.

But to go on from this to argue that universities should be required to set aside a quota of places for comprehensive school candidates *qua* comprehensive school candidates, is grotesque. Universities are places where people study academic subjects, or learn professional skills, to a certain final standard. In Britain they do so in the extremely short time of three years.

Unless one is willing to accept either a lengthening of the course or a drop in final standards (that is to say the production of less well-qualified doctors, lawyers, architects, engineers, economists, teachers or whatever), one must demand a certain level of preparation from entrants to the course. Independent schools must at least try to teach pupils up to this standard—if they are seen too conspicuously to fail, they go under.

Pressure on comprehensive schools to achieve the same standards is, for a variety of reasons, less. Under Professor Peston's proposed arrangements (with what a note of tender pride he pronounces the words 'my quota scheme'!), it would vanish altogether.

But one feels that mundane arguments about things like standards, numbers, costs, incentives, are powerless against the Utopian, or Orwellian, reasoning of such as Professor Peston.

The Times Educational Supplement, 4 June 1976.

Professor Peston writes in his introduction to Hunter Davies's *The Creighton Report* (1976): 'Despite the theoretical arguments showing the desirability of comprehensive education, and the welter of statistics proving how successful these schools have been, the debate concerning their future still goes on.' What statistics? Professor Peston does not mention that comprehensives cannot equal the examination successes of the old bipartite system (see Baldwin's article pp. 62–68). If he denies this, if there are 'a welter of statistics', why is the Labour Party so determined that they

should not be published? What is the Labour Party doing about the fact that in at least one London comprehensive school in 1975 there was not one O-level pass?

Mixed ability teaching

The crucial issue for the next few years is likely to be mixed ability teaching. If this is allowed to spread through the comprehensive schools, standards will be lowered even further, our economic future will be irretrievably damaged, and our culture debased. There is no evidence that mixed ability teaching can maintain standards. The reason is simple. Hunter Davies writes in *The Creighton Report*: 'Teaching a mixed ability group can be very rewarding and, if done properly, can benefit both the slow and the fast learners. All it means is that you work twice as hard.'

In other words it will not work with the normal teacher. Any system that demands twice as much work from teachers must fail. The strain of teaching is considerable in the usual conditions without adding the burden of mixed ability classes. In a review of *The Creighton Report*, Woodrow Wyatt commented:

At Creighton, and many other comprehensives, mixed-ability classes are the ideal and norm. The brighter children must work mingled with the dimmer, despite the nightmare strain on teachers trying to deal with wildly disparate elements at the same time, otherwise all would not be equal. However, the unreconstructed Mr Hasdell, the Head of English, after trying the mixed-ability rubbish for two years insisted on dropping it.

Now, for English, the children are divided by aptitude so that in last year's O-levels 50 fifth-form entrants out of 52 passed English Language and 37 out of 38 passed English Literature against a national average of 65 per cent. A similar revolt in the Maths department has produced similar results.

Observer, 23 May 1976.

Mixed ability teaching is the ideal that animates many supporters of the new 16 plus examination. C. H. Lawrence wrote in *The Times:*

The fact is, this is only the latest of a whole

series of ill-judged schemes which the Schools Council has sponsored in an attempt to modify or destroy the existing system of school-leaving examinations. It all too clearly reflects the pre-occupation of the educational theory establishment with socio-political issues rather than with educational standards. Happily, most of the kites the council has flown (at much public expense) have been shot down in time, though one at least got through and continues to pose a problem for those who have the task of awarding marks in the GCE examinations.

The chief objection raised against the existing system seems to be that it penalises weak candidates. The new scheme is well designed to penalise the strong ones. Moreover, it is likely to have damaging side-effects upon the organisation of teaching. Since all will be working towards one examination, those children with the aptitude and will to study who are at present taught in O-level groups, can be broken up and redistributed into so-called 'mixed ability' groups, to the educational disadvantage of all.

In order to solve the problem of the weak or bored pupil and the incompetent teacher, the scheme has come up with a device which is truly novel and daring. It permits alternative modes of examination, and under one of these a school which prefers not to be assessed by an independent board can opt to conduct its own examination. Thus Barchester Comprehensive need no longer suffer the indignity of having 70 per cent of its maths candidates failed year after year; it will now be able to step in and award a pass to all its pupils. It is understandable that this device should be popular with some members of the National Union of Teachers, but it is hard to see how such an examination could have any public validity.

The University Grants Committee has recently drawn attention to the alarming decline in general educational standards among university entrants over the last ten years. Many of us who are concerned with disciplines that require a grasp of maths or languages (and competence in languages is a skill needed by many students besides those who are studying for language degrees) consider that the UGC has, if anything, understated the gravity of the situation. It is disheartening that the only contribution that the Schools Council has to offer to meet this crisis should be a charlatans' charter.

The NUT reacts violently to suggestions that standardisation of marks will be impossible if teachers assess their own pupils. A recent report on middle schools, however, makes it clear that chaos will result:

> Some middle schools regard the study of a modern language as being of prime importance, while others do not. Some pupils arrive at senior school with a great deal of knowledge and expertise and others with little or none. Some middle schools are unable to recruit qualified staff while others are more fortunate and may even introduce the pupils to two modern languages.
>
> In many of the senior schools a disguised new start has to be made. One school claimed it had to do the usual first year work in the first term, the second year work in the second term and then, with any luck, it could start on the third year work in the summer term. . . .
>
> Most senior schools took pupils from five or six middle schools, but one senior school that was studied took pupils from no fewer than 40 middle schools. This school set tests in English and mathematics for all its future pupils.
>
> Other senior schools had much greater difficulty in assessing their new pupils. This was because there was considerable variation in the standards of different middle schools. And in an area where middle schools were asked to grade children on an A to E scale, one school never gave higher than a grade C while another gave an abundance of As.

The Times Educational Supplement, 7 May 1976.

Anyone who reads UCCA forms knows how widely head teachers vary in their optimism about their sixth formers. The end of a public examination system, with external objective assessment, will be the end of agreed standards. For obvious reasons mixed ability teaching with no external assessment will particularly damage working-class children.

Selection

In 1975 Stuart Maclure and Harry Judge came out for selection at 14 plus. After a visit to the States, Maclure reported that everyone said to him:

Do you seriously mean to say that Britain is on the point of getting rid of those first rate grammar schools? Why don't your politicians take the elementary trouble to learn from our mistakes in what has happened to the high school?
The Times Educational Supplement, April 1975.

He went on to argue for 14 plus selection, saying: 'there is good evidence that the full, unadulterated comprehensive gospel is not held by many in the educational world and by few except ardent party ideologists anywhere.'

In an article discussing the *Black Papers*, Harry Judge supported Maclure's proposal for comprehensive schooling only up to the age of 14:

It is idle to pretend that there survives—in secondary schools, in colleges and departments of education, in local education authorities, even in the hearts of bruised sociologists—any powerful conviction that the present phase of comprehensive planning will bring great educational improvement, or even be worth doing at all. A great deal of progress (and I mean progress) has been made, and now is the time for consolidation and settlement.
The Times Educational Supplement.

He continued: 'Nobody believes that an orthodox system of 11 to 18 comprehensive schools for all big cities even begins to make sense. Nor is it possible to dismiss as hostile propaganda the massive doubts so many people entertain about neighbourhood schools for all.'

In the Charles Gittins lecture at University College, Swansea, in 1976, Dr Judge specifically attacked the moves in comprehensives towards a common curriculum. The abridged version in *The Times Educational Supplement* reads:

When comprehensive schools were first established, a wide and free range of curriculum choice was one of their dominant selling points . . . But there now arises a new puritanism, hostile to such mindless promiscuity . . . To allow freedom of choice, save within authoritatively defined limits, is, the argument runs, to connive at deprivation.

From such tangled roots grows the presently flourishing doctrine of the common curriculum. . . . The efforts to define and apply it will vary . . . but all are bound to tend towards an

agreed, consensual, national understanding of a single and common curriculum. The characteristics of such a curriculum are certain to be a diluted intellectualism, hostility to the vocational, and a sham aestheticism.

Against such powerful tendencies towards uniformity should be set the wisdom of pursuing difference. Educationists, in particular, should recognise the right of the pupil not to be unnecessarily bored.

Pupils will, by the age of 14, have completed nine years of fundamental and compulsory education. For a growing number, all or most of that time will have been spent in mixed ability groups, following a programme of studies within which there is relatively little differentiation. Their tastes will have been to a great extent formed (or distorted).

It is hypocritical and unkind to pretend that either all or none of them wish to study two or more foreign languages, or spend substantial periods of time in a music school, or find excitement in project technology. . . . Pupils at the age of 14 often have a not unsatisfactory notion at least of the activities and subjects they wish to pursue . . . There are strict limits upon what they can all be required to do, and even stricter limits upon what they might all be reasonably expected to find interesting.

The choice is, therefore, between a doctrine of secondary education which stresses the uniformity of a common curriculum extending across five years (with doubtless, a common examination to prove that it all happened), and a general policy which, while acknowledging the virtues of an undifferentiated curriculum up to the age of 14, then permits a marked change of emphasis towards diversity and well-motivated choice.

By such compromises academic education may yet survive.

Conclusion

It is vital in secondary education that both the finest academic schooling for the intellectually gifted and a good general education for the academically less able should survive. It is against these aims that suggestions of middle schools, selection at fourteen and sixth form colleges must be assessed. There have already been too many mistakes in secondary school reorganisation, most of them now acknowledged. We can afford no more.

Sixth form selective colleges are likely to rob their 11–16 feed schools of their most able graduate staff, so that their scholarship will decline and no foundation be laid for the future A-level courses. Open access sixth form colleges are likely to be so diffused in their aims and interests that there will not be the sense of unity necessary for academic success.

Middle school systems will only be successful where the 13–18 upper schools control the curriculum of their 9–13 feed schools; otherwise too much time will be wasted in sorting out children from different courses two years before O-level. Additional changes of school are in any case of doubtful value since children must put down secure roots to succeed.

Selection at 14, as now advocated, when compared with selection at 11, will be much more of a handicap to the bright pupil from the deprived home attending up to that age a low achievement all-ability school in a poor neighbourhood. By then habits of not working, low standards and an anti-academic bias may have been irretrievably developed. He may not obtain or even desire selection at 14. It is the bright working-class pupils who have suffered most from comprehensive reorganisation.

The trouble with the large city comprehensive school is that there is generally no unity of ability, subject interest or community background. This undoubtedly weights the dice against their success. Why not let each comprehensive develop some speciality of subject course for which parents, via the methods proposed by Stuart Sexton, or the educational voucher, could opt? Mr Sexton's article on this is fascinating. Why not encourage the creation of technical comprehensive schools where all the intake has at least a unity arising from an interest in technical subjects, from pupils who will eventually read engineering degrees at university to technicians to craft apprentices? The article by Mr Vigars shows how few technical A-level options are now offered by London Comprehensive schools. It also shows how few comprehensives are comprehensive in the subjects offered. Why not face the fact and encourage subject specialisation in comprehensives so that some are mathematically based, some linguistically based, some scientifically orientated, etc.?

The ex-direct-grant schools once again reinstated into the state system could be elite academic schools to keep genuine scholarship alive. They could be like the elite schools of Russia and Eastern Europe and the USA. The subject-orientated schools might achieve a similar sense of unity and purpose.

If the latter failed, however, the local education authorities should re-establish selective (by ability) academic schools for 20 to 40 per cent of children. We cannot continue to handicap children for a barren political doctrine which will also further impoverish our country. The wheel will not come exactly full circle, for a revolution or counter-revolution never takes one back exactly to the same place. We must keep our options open, the very thing the left wing most fears. This shows their lack of faith in the effectiveness of their suggestions. We cannot, however, remain as we are with a monolithic, failing comprehensive system, if we are to preserve scholarship and survive as an economic community.

THE EDITORS

The dissolution of the grammar school

R. W. BALDWIN

Mr Mulley stubbed his toe against the law lords over Tameside, but his welcome successor, Mrs Williams, inherits his Bill to dissolve all maintained grammar schools, which will become law unless the House of Lords as a whole, supported by public opinion and, one trusts, some second thoughts from Mrs Williams herself, can bring some modification. This is why the latest evidence from the DES giving full results for 1974 and partial for 1975 is particularly relevant and opportune.

Broadly, the picture remains the same as that revealed last year in *The Great Comprehensive Gamble* (available from Independent Schools Information Service, 47 Victoria Street, London SW1, price 40p post free). In 1974, in the lower grades of the CSE, the modern schools did as well as or better than the comprehensives; at the starting level of O-level and CSE grade 1 (at least one pass), the modern schools still did very creditably (43 per cent of leavers had achieved this level of success), but the comprehensives were ahead (56 per cent). At the stage of 5 or more O-levels or CSE grade 1, the modern schools dropped back (5.6 per cent), and the comprehensives were 15 per cent, compared however with 22 per cent for the total selective sector (modern + grammar schools). For A-levels there are figures for both 1974 and 1975. Leavers with at least one A-level from the selective schools (grammar and secondary modern) were 14.7 per cent in 1974 and 15.6 per cent in 1975, and from the comprehensives 11.1 per cent and 11.0 per cent. For those with at least two A-levels the selective figures were 11.7 per cent and 12.6 per cent and for the comprehensives 8.2 per cent and 8.3 per cent, and for those with at least three A-levels they were 7.7 per cent and 8.5 per cent for the selective schools and 4.9 per cent and 5.0 per cent for the comprehensives.

At the other end of the scale, the proportion who left school with no paper qualifications at all fell from 23 to 22 per cent in the comprehensives, from 21 to 19 per cent in the selective schools, and from 27 to 24 per cent in the modern schools taken on their own.

I will return to these comparisons after dealing with creaming, but first let us look at the total for all maintained schools together, since these are free of any creaming distortion. Compared with 1966, when comprehensives were only 11 per cent of the total against 67 per cent in 1975, percentage successes have changed as follows:

	At least 1 CSE pass	5 or more CSE passes	At least 1 O-level or CSE grade 1	5 or more O levels or CSE grade 1	At least 1 A level	At least 2 A levels	At least 3 A levels
1966	16.15	4.82	36.28	17.23	10.88	8.52	5.42
1969	30.11	12.33	44.81	18.13	12.56	9.59	6.04
1970	33.63	14.30	47.55	18.34	12.90	10.02	6.06
1971	34.84	15.37	48.22	18.65	13.68	10.52	6.51
1972	37.20	16.98	49.88	18.37	13.24	10.11	6.34
1973	Comparisons invalidated by raising of school leaving age						
1974	61.45	23.42	58.20	17.84	12.54	9.61	6.01
1975	*	*	*	*	12.51	9.69	6.17

* Figures not yet available.

The introduction of CSE in the mid 60s, combined with the raising of the school leaving age in 1972, produced the big increases in the first 3 columns. At the level however of five or more O-levels and one or more A-levels, the percentages after rising to a peak in 1971 have fallen with a slight upturn for two and three A-level passes in 1975, principally in the maintained grammar schools.

These figures are for passes in all subjects, but for many purposes some subjects are more essential than others, mathematics, for instance, than

general studies. The statistics of passes in separate subjects include passes by students in colleges of further education, but at A-level these can be taken out, so as to leave the numbers of passes in particular subjects by school leavers only. In this context it is important to look at boys and girls separately, since the latter have shown an overall advance in these years of catching up to the boys' levels. The figures give passes per 100 school leavers in both summer and winter examinations, including any duplicate passes in successive years.

		Modern languages	Maths	Natural sciences	Social science and vocational	Total subjects
Boys	1965	3.55	10.14	15.04	7.93	47.13
	1971	3.07	10.44	14.55	11.44	52.30
	1974	2.53	8.65	13.67	11.44	47.55
Girls	1965	4.60	1.98	5.13	3.37	27.02
	1971	5.80	3.04	6.29	6.83	38.91
	1974	4.97	2.65	6.55	7.38	36.82

Thus the girls' performance rose markedly from 1965 to 1971, since when it has fallen in modern languages and mathematics, while the boys' performance in these two groups of subjects has fallen more noticeably; it has also fallen in the natural science group.

These figures are for all schools including Direct Grant and Independent, which in A-levels are responsible for about 28 per cent of boys' passes by school leavers. In such DG schools as I have consulted, there has been no or less fall in these three groups of academic subjects (modern languages, maths and natural sciences) over this ten years, and insofar as much the same may be true of most DG and Independent Schools, this implies that the percentage fall in these subjects in the maintained schools has been somewhat greater than that shown in the table. It is also very possible that the maintained grammar schools have kept up the proportion of passes in these subjects better than the comprehensives, and if so this would further affect the latters' percentages.

Creaming

This suggestion of differential performance by grammar and comprehensive schools in particular subjects brings us back to the different levels of performance generally as summarised above. The crude differences are undoubtedly affected by

some degree of creaming of comprehensives by maintained grammar schools (i.e. in mixed areas such as the ILEA the pupils entering the comprehensives do not include a representative spread over the whole range of ability, because the selective sector, still containing in 1974 and 1975 many esteemed grammar schools, attracts more than the average proportion of grammar school-type pupils). The great majority of Authorities are now in process of transition; in a few areas in 1974 there were only comprehensives and grammar schools (maximum creaming), in a few others there were only comprehensives and modern schools (creaming away from the selective to the comprehensive sector). The problem is to estimate the importance of this factor. In the present rapidly changing situation the only guide is the overall percentage of grammar school pupils in the selective sector, but even with this there are complications. Which is the best criterion of the three sets of figures available—those of leavers, those of pupils aged 13, or those of all secondary pupils? The index usually quoted is that for leavers, because the performance figures relate to them, but in recent years the pupils in modern schools have been staying on longer, which depresses the number of their leavers and thereby increases the grammar school percentage. Conversely the figures of total pupils show the opposite fault, since as the modern school pupils stay on longer this increases their total numbers in school and depresses the grammar school percentage.

The safest figure to take is that for pupils aged 13, which escapes both distortions.

There is however another factor, namely the technical schools. These have now virtually disappeared, but 10 years ago were not unimportant, and authorities such as Manchester which had good technical schools tended to have low grammar school percentages. From the point of view of judging any change in the composition of the pupils in the selective sector, it is arguably preferable to take grammar and technical together for comparison with secondary modern.

The following table shows how these various percentages have changed over the last 25 years, during which the proportion of 13-year-olds in comprehensive schools has risen from under 1 per cent in the fifties to 8 per cent in 1965 and 61 per cent in 1974 (leavers 67 per cent in 1975).

Percentages of grammar or grammar plus technical pupils of the total pupils in maintained selective schools in England and Wales

	Leavers		Total pupils		Pupils aged 13	
	Grammar only	Grammar + Technical	Grammar only	Grammar + Technical	Grammar only	Grammar + Technical
1950	20.02	25.46	29.80	34.10	23.95	28.23
1955	19.39	24.84	27.83	32.43	22.39	27.22
1960	19.53	23.68	25.94	29.87	20.01	23.47
1965	22.53	25.58	27.86	31.14	21.28	24.01
1966	22.87	25.52 E	28.47	31.40	22.12	24.61
1972	26.01	27.78 E	28.21	29.95	23.44	24.99
1974	27.30	28.76 E	29.08	30.58	25.11	26.43
1975	27.16	*	*	*	*	*

* Figures not yet available; E = Estimated

There was a fall in grammar percentage during the fifties because it took time for local education authorities to provide more grammar schools to cope with the great increase in numbers. The proportion rose in the sixties, before comprehensives were significant, as grammar school provision was increased, and reached a peak (as a percentage of pupils aged 13 in all maintained schools) in 1966. Since then creaming has become a factor, but it will be seen that on the best criterion, pupils aged 13, the percentage has risen by under 3 per cent. For leavers only the increase was between 3 and 5 per cent depending on whether technical schools are included, and for total pupils there was either a small increase or decrease.

Using the 3 per cent figure based on pupils aged 13, the relative performance figures can be corrected for creaming by transferring from the grammar schools to the comprehensives 3 per cent of the selective sector pupils (7,750 in 1974 and 6,384 in 1975, crediting the comprehensives with these grammar pupils' successes at the grammar school rates, and similarly debiting the selective sector figures), and recalculating the respective percentages accordingly. This gives the following adjusted successes per 100 leavers:

		At least 5 O-levels inc. CSE grade 1	At least 1 A-level	At least 2 A-levels	At least 3 A-levels
1974	Comprehensive	16.03	11.80	8.79	5.31
	Selective (grammar and secondary modern)	20.64	13.70	10.87	7.11
1975	Comprehensive	*	11.59	8.76	5.36
	Selective (grammar and secondary modern)	*	14.51	11.68	7.90

* Figures not yet available.

Against this statistical evidence let us rehearse some of the claims made, and then try to estimate what is actually happening, what will probably happen if the Government's policy is pursued to its conclusion, and what other course might suggest itself.

(I have not quoted any local figures to supplement those above for England and Wales as a whole, because very few are available publicly. Suffice it to state that none that I have seen, some in confidence, contradict or affect the national evidence.)

The claims and the result

The whole campaign for the replacement of the selective by the comprehensive system has been based on two main arguments. The House of Commons motion of 21 January 1965 referred to the 'need to raise educational standards at all levels' which 'is impeded by the separation of children into different types of secondary schools'. A year later the Secretary of State for Education, Mr Anthony Crosland, addressing the North of England Educational Conference on 7 January 1966 (reprinted in *Socialism Now* 1974) held that the 'central and irresistible argument against the 11 plus lies in the denial of social justice and equal opportunity that it implies' because the 11 plus reflected not only IQ but also environmental factors, especially home and neighbourhood and parental aspirations. He went on to refer to the fallibility and arbitrariness of selection, and the 'frightful waste of latent talent through the sheer fact of segregation, through the discouragement put upon a large group of the population by the label of failure'. For these and such reasons he believed 'the tripartite or bipartite system to be educationally and socially unjust, inefficient, wasteful and divisive'.

The evidence above surely indicates that so far at least the switch to comprehensives has not raised educational performance. The big rise in figures for CSE has been due mainly to the rapid growth of that examination, and to the raising of the school leaving age which has encouraged many more to sit. This is proved by the fact that the remaining modern schools have shown equally dramatic increases. At the more academic levels of qualification for higher education—five or more O-levels, or one or more A-levels—all schools,

selective and comprehensive, have advanced equally, and the selective schools have stayed well ahead even after allowing for creaming. The failure of the efficiency argument entails also at least a substantial revision of the social justice argument. If the academic performance levels of comprehensive schools are on average not higher, but lower, than those of selective schools, any lessening of social injustice can only be the ironing out of differences by levelling down, not levelling up. Some pupils indeed who might have failed the 11 plus may do better in a comprehensive, but if total results are no better and probably lower, their gain must be balanced by more loss to others who do worse.

In his prediction of the comprehensive Utopia, Mr Crosland went on to refer to academic subjects such as mathematics. 'There is some evidence that in mathematics at least the bright pre-university pupils in countries with a comprehensive system do just as well as pupils in a highly selective system such as ours. Moreover, to support this point, the mathematics performance of pupils of lower ability is much higher in the comprehensive countries than in selective countries'. Compare this prediction with the figures above showing the decline in boys' passes per head at A-level over the last 10 years, a decline not shared by direct grant schools.

As to the reasons for these disappointments, I think Mr Crosland himself unintentionally indicated one important factor. 'We all know that standards in a school are partly set by what sociologists call the student culture, by the young taste-makers and opinion-moulders. If these are hostile to brains, to school and to teacher, the intellectual standards will be low. But to the extent that an academic stream exists, setting at least one model and acting as intellectual pace-maker, to that extent the standard will improve'. This is a good objective, but is there not a great danger that the predominant student culture in many comprehensives, as much as in some modern schools, will be hostile to brains, so that the academic stream will be the victim, rather than the leaven, of the school environment?

In this field generalisation is dangerous if not impossible. When whole areas go over from one system to the other, the pupils and staff, with their abilities and limitations, interests and aspirations, remain the same but change from one grouping to another. The functional organisation is replaced by mainly geographical grouping into larger units, within each of which the constituents, pupils and staff, form a new amalgam whose culture and performance will depend on the nature, quality and potentiality of all the components. The spread of IQ among the pupils, their cultural and social backgrounds, the academic and pedagogic quality of the head and staff, will cover the whole range of permutations and combinations. Some schools in fortunate areas with good staff will give all pupils, from the brightest to the slowest, an education well suited to their abilities and interests, with an adequate range of subjects in the sixth form for academic and non-academic pupils alike and reasonable economy of teaching staff. Other schools with fewer advantages of neighbourhood but outstanding staff will also achieve good results. Others again may never break out of the sort of student attitudes mentioned by Mr Crosland, and in such schools the able pupils will be vastly worse off (at great social injustice) than in a grammar school, while the non-academic may also have less chance than in a good modern school of having their own requirements specifically studied and met. To quote from the Leader of the Opposition in the ILEA (letter in *The Times* 31 August 1976): 'In Inner London many comprehensives are comprehensive in name only; they provide neither a "technical" education nor a "modern" education, but only that of a third-rate grammar school of an almost Dickensian character' (see Mr Vigars's article, pp. 68–71).

There are at least two other vital factors influencing the situation. First, the disappearance of the 11 plus is increasingly admitted as a cause of lowered standards at the point of entry to secondary school. This was shown by Dr Bennett's recent research, and is further reflected in details provided by Alfred Levy on pp. 23–29 of this *Black Paper.*

Second is the constant problem of combining variety and efficiency at A-levels. Unless a comprehensive is large enough to have an academic sixth form as large as the average grammar school, which means that it must be three or four times as big in total, it cannot throw up teaching groups of economic size except for the few most popular subjects. Therefore the range of subjects is cut

down, and even so there are a great many teaching groups of absurdly and wastefully low size, some down to one pupil only. (How many local education authorities know, or care, what is the average size of A-level teaching groups in their sixth forms? Yet when qualified academic staff are teaching one or two pupils only, they are not available for teaching larger groups in earlier years on which A-level work depends.) This situation probably explains in part why the percentage of pupils taking A-levels in modern languages has fallen so markedly in the last 10 years. The Classical languages of course are fast dying out except in the DG and Independent Schools; Latin has severely shrunk, and Greek virtually gone. They may be largely irrelevant, like much history and literature, to the current needs of the British economy, but at the high risk of derision I deplore that the language of Homer, Thucydides, Sophocles, Plato and Aristotle, the quarry for so much of our own tongue, comparable only with English and French for its richness and flexibility of expression and the quality of its literature, is now closed to all except fee-paying children.

Sixth-form colleges are proposed and are being increasingly adopted as an answer to this problem, but they have the great disadvantage of disrupting students' education at a critical stage, and of depriving the majority of teachers of A-level or other sixth-form teaching. They may well be the best solution to this organisational difficulty, but the solution with its inherent disadvantages is itself a by-product of the comprehensive system.

The Education Bill

If this is enacted without substantial amendment, the present process of dissolution of the maintained grammar schools will be complete within a few years. As they and their pupils are absorbed or translated into the comprehensives, the figures for comprehensives will tend to rise, simply as a matter of statistics, to the average for all maintained schools. The test will be what happens to that average over the next 5 to 7 years—whether it will rise, or stabilise at the present level, somewhat below 1971, or show a further fall. And more important than the total average will be the performance in key subjects such as maths, natural sciences and modern languages. The evidence so far gives absolutely no justification for confidence and plenty for apprehension.

There is an immense fund of goodwill and determination among teachers and LEAs to make a success of reorganisation, but problems and difficulties do not go away because they are awkward and unpopular. Instead they may be swept under the carpet, and statistics manipulated to hide the true situation. Consider for instance Mr Mulley's speech to the Society of Education Officers (Press release of 22 January 1976). 'There is no evidence of any kind that educational standards are falling as a result of secondary reorganisation'. After quoting percentages for those achieving one to four O-levels—not a very significant figure since it excluded pupils going on to A-levels, and was in any case greatly influenced by the growth of CSE and by ROSLA—(more useful figures were given in the first table above), he went on: 'A-level results have also been encouraging. In 1964 2.1 per cent of leavers (from all schools) passed in one subject; in 1974 the figure was 3.3 per cent. At the same time, the percentage of leavers who passed in three or more subjects rose from 5.5 per cent to 7.9 per cent. This rise has taken place in a comparatively short space of time—only 10 years'.) Whoever would have guessed from these remarks that the entire increase quoted had already occurred during the first part of this period and that in the more recent years, when the switch to comprehensives had assumed massive dimensions, there had been a decline? Was this 'the truth, the whole truth and nothing but the truth' in the mouth of a Minister recently pleading his Tameside case before the highest legal tribunal, or was it 'the halting tongue that dares not tell the whole'?

The future

Mr Mulley showed himself able and willing at the recent CLEA conference in Manchester to stand up for common sense in finance. Pray that his successor will be equally prepared to stand up for common sense on this reorganisation issue. Surely the fact is that there are great arguments of sentiment and superficial equality for the comprehensive approach, but great arguments of efficiency and real benefit in the functional, selective approach. What we all want is the best education for all (within the limits of what the public are prepared to pay for the education service), whether future leaders of industry, commerce or the professions, or future managers, or skilled or less skilled workers, or housewives and mothers. Those with higher IQs can study more subjects more quickly and intensively, up to the frontiers of knowledge and practice, and should be encouraged in their own and the country's interests to do so. At some stage they must be selected, and whether at 11, or a little later by streaming in comprehensives, or on entry to higher education, is a matter on which many opinions can be held. We now have a plethora of alternatives in the maintained system, and the sensible course is to study what is actually happening in each case, and hope to discover the best, but preferably always leave some variety among good practice.

The creaming bogey can be eliminated by leaving some areas completely selective—especially when as at Tameside the majority of voters prefer this—for comparison with others completely comprehensive. This need not and should not mean that the non-academic schools in selective areas are regarded as filled with failures, or as inferior in any respect. These schools, indeed, many of which are excellent and show up well in examination results (see above), should be the centre of development, on the lines suggested by the Chairman of the Schools Council, Sir Alex Smith, at the recent British Association meeting, for integrating school education by sandwich courses, day-release, apprenticeships, or otherwise, with instruction in the skills, techniques and requirements of the working world outside.

Nor need the alleged arbitrariness of the 11 plus be an obstacle. There should always be full flexibility for transfer both ways, and at the time of selection itself there might be an intermediate boundary area where allocations to one or other type of school are made after consultation with staff and parents. It should not be a question of success or failure, but on the one hand an academic type of education with plenty of openings towards technology, production and commerce on which the country's life depends, and on the other hand a more technical, practical kind of education, including the essential grounding in the three Rs and the cultivation of good citizenship and enjoyment of leisure, always with the opportunity of moving to the academic schools if pupils wish and can benefit by it.

An appeal

This therefore is an appeal to the new Secretary of State to face facts, all the facts, objectively and patiently, and to accept that the present evidence, while not without its brighter spots, is in total at best inconclusive, and soberly viewed, is disappointing if not alarming in certain respects. It is an appeal for goodwill, common sense, and a readiness to welcome diversity at this stage and perhaps permanently, so that in the common desire to provide the best conditions for all children, we can allow the full potential of each system, practised and developed as wisely and flexibly as possible, to emerge with fuller experience.

How comprehensive?

ROBERT VIGARS

How comprehensive are the generality of comprehensive schools? Are the courses and the teaching formerly available at the grammar school, the modern school and the technical school available to every pupil at every comprehensive? It is important that they should be so available for two reasons if the comprehensive system as at present conceived is to survive; if they are not available and unlikely to become available, then the system is at fault and must be changed.

First, however much lip service is paid to parental choice, the choice of school at 11 plus has in practice become increasingly limited by locality: outside the major cities, there may be only one, or at best two large schools within reach, or at which pupils from a given area will be accepted. In the cities and conurbations, restrictions to avoid oversubscription of particular schools will invariably narrow the choice in practice to far fewer schools than may on paper appear to be available.

Secondly, the pupil who develops a particular aptitude or ability is no longer encouraged to attend a school offering specialist courses to meet his needs: he and his parents are encouraged instead to believe that his local comprehensive is truly comprehensive or, if he has a choice, that each and every school is equally suitable. So by the accident of geography or by the workings of a system of choice or allocation unrelated to the availability or strength of particular courses the child finds himself in his comprehensive school. If he needs a strong technical department, will he find it? Or modern languages? Or maths and science? Or art? How comprehensive is his comprehensive?

Even in a world where there were no shortages of teaching skills in specialised subjects, and no shortage of finance to make good deficiencies of particular equipment or facilities arising from historic causes, it seems unlikely from the nature of things (or perhaps from the nature of head teachers!) that every school should be equally strong in every department. But in the world as we know it, so much the more unreal is that ideal.

A whole generation of children has passed through comprehensive schools where there have been few teachers qualified to teach maths or science subjects at all, or where the technical department has been unable to rise above junior woodwork and metalwork, or where the laboratories, or the art rooms, or the workshops have been grossly inadequate.

It is no answer to hope that these are temporary difficulties or inadequacies. In the first place, that is small comfort for the child whose years at school are equally 'temporary'—or contemporary with the period of difficulty. But is it not more likely that as fast as one difficulty is overcome, another will appear?

It is no answer either to place one's faith in any of the latest palliative gimmicks: sixth form colleges, sixth form centres, cooperative sixth forms or college-linked courses. A specialism cannot develop at sixth form level if the groundwork is missing. The sixth form courses may be made available by the devices mentioned, or perhaps by others, but they will be starved of students if the course lacks the sub-structure of basic work in a properly equipped and fully staffed department at lower levels.

Let us see how this works out in Inner London. The Inner London Education Authority (ILEA) has some 133,500 pupils in 123 comprehensive schools. Out of those 123 schools the numbers able to offer A-level courses in the technical subjects listed below in 1975/76 were as follows:

technical drawing (including engineering drawing and geometrical drawing)	38
woodwork	5
metalwork	13
engineering	2
engineering science	nil
design and technology	13

It emerges from these figures that less than a quarter of Inner London's 123 comprehensives were able to offer a course in even one A-level technical subject, and only about one in ten was able to offer more than one subject. What right had the remainder to the title 'comprehensive'?

The total number of sixth-formers throughout Inner London working at each subject at the beginning of the academic year (out of a total secondary comprehensive school roll of 133,500) was:

technical drawing	213
woodwork	11
metalwork	48
engineering	7
engineering science	nil
design and technology	58

When challenged at a meeting of the Education Committee to say whether these figures were satisfactory in view of the claims of the comprehensives to offer courses suitable for the aptitude of every pupil, and in view of the absorption by the comprehensives of the many excellent technical schools previously in Inner London, the Chairman of the Schools Sub-Committee replied:

All secondary comprehensive schools of this Authority are pledged and determined *to attempt to provide* for all the innate abilities,

interests and aptitudes of their pupils. The extent to which they are able to do so is dependent upon a large number of other factors which are outside the control of the Authority. I am satisfied that all our secondary comprehensive schools in cooperation with colleges of further education and in cooperation with each other *seek to meet* the real and expressed aims and ambitions and aptitudes of all those pupils on their roll.

The operative words here are *attempt to provide* and *seek to meet*. The extent to which they succeed in technical subjects is shown by the preceding tables.

There will be those who will say that sixth-form courses in technical subjects are not relevant to the needs of industry and to those seeking employment in industry, in so far as apprentices will be leaving school at 16, and for those staying at school longer with a view to entering higher education, subjects such as maths and science are more important. Not so: it is the very lack of sufficient practical emphasis in their education that hampers our engineers, technologists and technicians. Moreover, where are we to find the technical teachers of the future if teaching in technical subjects stops at 16? And in the absence of sixth-form courses, technical departments will always be seen as the poor relations, and technical work held in low esteem by pupils and their parents. There is an echo here of the old arguments on 'parity of esteem' under the tripartite structure of schools. Parity has not been achieved in the comprehensives of Inner London. The argument has just been brushed under the carpet: for the pupil the problem has been accentuated by the disappearance of the good specialist technical schools.

Turning from technical studies to the more general subject groups of mathematics, science and modern languages the provision of courses throughout Inner London is again sporadic. For certain administrative purposes, Inner London is divided into 10 Divisions. The table below shows the distribution of A-level courses in the comprehensive schools of these 10 Divisions. The figures are quite startling and again give the lie to the description 'comprehensive'. In many schools maths, sciences and languages are not taught up to A-level standard.

Distribution of A-level courses in Comprehensive schools in Inner London's 10 Administrative Divisions: September 1975

Division	Comprehensive schools	Pure maths		Other maths		Biology		Physics		Chemistry		French		German		Spanish		Comprehensive schools teaching 3 or more modern languages at A-level
		schools	pupils	schools	pupils	schools	pupils	schools	pupils	schools	pupils	schools	pupils	schools	pupils	schools	pupils	
1	16	6	45	8	111	11	76	9	94	8	95	9	80	2	7	5	35	3
2	18	8	58	10	151	14	214	13	165	13	151	13	125	7	31	4	18	4
3	12	5	87	4	60	8	69	6	94	5	59	5	43	—	—	1	1	2
4	14	7	50	5	29	10	59	10	60	9	63	8	60	3	20	—	—	1
5	15	11	54	2	6	9	50	6	40	7	32	4	22	2	11	1	4	—
6	17	7	142	8	181	8	118	10	152	10	125	7	82	5	14	3	9	2
7	14	7	75	5	69	10	87	8	91	9	75	9	73	2	10	—	—	—
8	20	9	79	9	72	14	81	10	62	10	48	9	41	1	5	—	—	—
9	11	4	44	6	54	8	59	8	79	7	89	5	35	3	18	1	1	2
10	17	8	48	9	168	11	165	11	166	10	173	11	80	5	8	1	5	1

NOTE: Seven subjects comprise the 'other maths' column. It is therefore possible that the pupil numbers quoted contain an element of double counting.

The pupil numbers quoted relate to all pupils studying the subject at A-level in 1st, 2nd and 3rd year of the sixth form.

Redistribution of the pupils, the teachers and the courses from the reorganised selective schools to the remainder will not go very far to remedy the deficiencies shown by the table. Its principal consequence will be to accentuate another disastrous feature of the comprehensive system—the uneconomic deployment of specialist teachers to very small groups of sixth-form pupils. How small these groups are can be seen from the table, and it must be borne in mind in analysing these facts that the number of pupils in each subject group aggregates pupils pursuing a 2-year or even 3-year course, and may also in some subjects aggregate sub-groups within the group.

So we see that in the comprehensive schools of Inner London, many are without adequate technical departments, many without A-level maths, many without strong modern language departments. How comprehensive, then, are these comprehensives?

Even the intelligent, inquiring parent knowing what to look for and what questions to ask, and with plenty of time to ask them, will have difficulty in assessing the departmental weaknesses of particular schools. Even those who can make the assessment will find their choice circumscribed for the reasons outlined at the commencement of this article. But for the generality of parents, a comprehensive is a comprehensive is a comprehensive, and great is their dismay to find in the later years of their children's school career that the opportunities which they thought to be available, from years of propaganda, are just not there.

If the tide against the large comprehensive is now flowing as strongly as Mrs Shirley Williams herself acknowledged at a Press Conference shortly after her appointment, it is all the more urgent to encourage the schools to develop specialist interests, and to ensure (so far as geography and density of population allow) that parents have a real choice between schools offering a diversity of specialist interests. Any school developing in this way must combine with its specialism a basic course of comprehensive educa-

tion with such options as circumstances and resources permit.

Recruitment of highly qualified and experienced teachers to match the specialism should become easier as a natural consequence of its existence and development: the specialist staff will gravitate to the appropriate schools. In addition it would become the deliberate policy of the education authority to ensure so far as possible the development of the specialism by the allocation of appropriate resources and staff. The education authority would also have an important role in co-ordinating the development of the specialisms to ensure an even geographical spread and availability.

This does not represent a disguised return to the old tripartite system of modern, technical and grammar schools. In the first place, there will be a much greater flexibility of courses and specialisms, and each school will be free to develop in its own way, subject to coordination by the education authority as already indicated. Secondly, intake will be in accordance with parental choice influenced by the aptitude, rather than the ability, of the child. Thirdly, every school will provide a basic course of comprehensive education to a high standard.

None the less, the problem of matching aptitudes and schools—children and courses—will still be acute. There can be no return to selection at 11 plus. A three-tier system of primary school (5–9), middle school (9–13), and high school (13–18) ensures that the choice of senior school is made at an age when it can be exercised by both child and parent in a meaningful way in relation to the child's more developed aptitudes and in relation to the choice of courses which must in any event be made at the age of 13.

In the absence of a three-tier system, a change of school at 13 plus must be made a real option by administrative arrangements. It would be assisted perhaps by a more clear cut organisation of Lower and Upper School in the all-through (11–18) secondary school.

Is education compulsory?

JOHN PRICE

In common with most teachers I have believed for many years that although the 1944 Act does not compel persons of 'compulsory school age' to attend school there is an obligation upon their parents to ensure that they receive an education. Section 36, 'It shall be the duty of the parent of every child of compulsory school age to cause him to receive efficient full-time education suitable to his age, ability, and aptitude, either by regular attendance at school or otherwise.' From the voluntary nature of school attendance arises the unwritten 'school contract' whereby the parent undertakes to send his child to school with the right attitude of mind to enable the school to fulfil its part of the contract—namely to provide an education. My personal experience as a headmaster during the last two years, and a closer reading of the Act, have led me to the view that there is considerable doubt as to whether absolute compulsion exists in the law relating to education in England and Wales. If indeed there is no absolute obligation upon parents to ensure that their children are given efficient education then there is considerable implication for maintained schools, especially those struggling to contain senior pupils who have no wish to be in school.

On 18 September 1974 (my fourteenth day as a newly appointed headmaster) I had occasion to suspend a pupil whom I shall call Boy One. This boy had been made to wait outside my study after attacking another pupil. During this waiting period he intercepted a small boy passing by and gave him a message purporting to come from myself asking for his victim to come to see me. Believing the message to be genuine, the victim's teacher sent the boy to my study. Before he reached my door Boy One savagely attacked him for the second time, beating him about the body and kicking him in the head. The suspension had no disciplinary effect whatsoever as it subsequently became an 'indefinite suspension', Boy One neither being made to return to school nor having his name deleted from the school's admission register. For his acts of thuggery Boy One was rewarded with a leave ticket which enabled him to spend the last six months of his 'compulsory school age' away from school boasting of his exploits.

One week after the first suspension Boy Two qualified for the same treatment. This boy had a little while earlier blown cigarette smoke into a teacher's face and physically assaulted the same teacher. On the day I suspended Boy Two he had attacked another pupil to whom he had previously said, 'One day they're going to find you with a knife in your back.' The attack so terrified the poor lad that he fled the school. I asked for the boy to be expelled by the local education authority and the governors unanimously made the same request. The requests were rejected and I was obliged to keep Boy Two on my admission register. Although an attempt was made to provide home tuition for this boy from resources external to the school, by the time it was arranged it was too late and so did not take place. Boy Two had obviously won a leave ticket and licence to disregard authority. He too spent the final six months of his 'compulsory school age' doing precisely as he pleased, while still a pupil of my school!

Now it so happens that I believe a school without discipline is nothing, and had said so at my interview prior to appointment. It has been with some puzzlement, if not vexation, that I have observed these young thugs getting away scot free after committing offences of the utmost enormity. A state of affairs where victims go uncompensated and assailants go unpunished does not accord with my view of justice. Consequently I began to look much more closely at the manner in which the LEA was approaching these difficult cases of boys who had passed beyond the school's control, and the support given by the education officers, and indeed the LEA itself, to my colleagues and myself. A few years ago we were hearing about the 'limbo kids' of Birmingham—those pupils who had been suspended from school and against whom no further action was being taken. It seemed that we were having a similar situation in Kent.

The fact that a pupil is suspended from school does not remove from a parent the obligation imposed by Section 36 of the 1944 Act to secure an education for his offspring. Section 37(1) requires a local education authority to serve a notice upon the parent requiring him to comply with Section 36, if he is not so doing. However Section 37(2) says in effect that if after the serving of such a notice the local education authority is still not satisfied that the parent is complying with Section 36 it need take no further action against the parent if in the opinion of the local education authority it is not expedient that the child [sic] should attend school. Thus we appear to have a law with a perfect loophole. Thou shalt cause thy son to be educated but no one will compel you to do so.

By November 1974 a third boy at the school had learnt in his own way that in spite of Section 36 a loophole permits pupils to escape schooling. Boy Three systematically set out to defy the authority of the school, commonly assaulted one of the teachers and so viciously attacked a younger boy that he required hospital treatment. Understandably the younger boy was too frightened to return to school and resumed his education in a school several miles away. With police present to give me protection Boy Three was put out of the school. We heard that this particular boy took paid employment while still of compulsory school age. On the day prior to his going a teacher had prudently recorded in the boy's file the following comment. 'Boy Three has expressed to me in conversation recently his desire to be suspended. The fact that he is at present still on probation does not seem to bother him. As suspension is his obvious objective I have been racking my brains for an alternative. The only possible one is extraction from all lessons, but I am doubtful as to whether this will meet any objective of ours. In the end I regret to believe that suspension may be the only course and, therefore, in my opinion the boy "wins".' A second teacher had written in the same file, '. . . . I told him such behaviour could only get him into serious trouble to which he replied, "Go on suspend me, that's what I would like".' Boy Three did indeed win. No legal action was taken

by the LEA and the boy escaped the last four months of what is euphemistically termed 'compulsory education'.

It is little wonder that during this time I was beginning to learn that in certain cases, suspension, far from being a disciplinary act, was a licence to disregard authority, and that the young thug playing his cards correctly is able to secure for himself a legal leave ticket to freedom—but a leave ticket which can only be secured by the school being put in a gravely difficult position. It is rather akin to a prisoner winning his freedom not by good behaviour but by bad behaviour.

Just as one swallow does not make a summer so three suspension cases do not necessarily illustrate a loophole in the law. It took a further two cases to convince me that in England and Wales education is not absolutely compulsory because there is no obligation upon an LEA to serve a 'school attendance order' if in the opinion of the authority it is not expedient that a particular pupil should attend school. Clearly this question of 'authority opinion' is central to the whole issue. No guidelines are suggested as to how this opinion should be arrived at. For example in the case of our three boys the LEA did not ask the headmaster or teachers whether in their view it was expedient that the three boys should attend school. In fact the 'authority opinion' was not declared to the school, and an anomalous situation seemed to arise whereby the authority on the one hand tried to get the boys into other schools while at the same time ignoring the unequivocally clear requirement of Section 37(2) to serve upon the parents a school attendance order.

By March 1975 a fourth boy felt the time had come to throw over the traces. Coming from a family who had been a source of trouble to the police, and with a police record himself it was no surprise to us when the boy made it clear that he did not intend to accept my authority any more. After he threatened me with physical violence I suspended Boy Four. The parents refused to communicate with the school, answered no letters, and failed to attend a suspensions panel meeting called to consider the matter. The boy's severance with the school was complete. He enjoyed an extra four months' idleness that year.

In December 1975 a teacher reported to me the intolerable behaviour of Boy Five who had previously been a considerable nuisance in the school. Boy Five made it quite clear one day that not only would he no longer accept the authority of the complaining teacher but he would not accept orders from myself either. He left me with the impression that he had deliberately chosen that particular day to gain his freedom. The usual indefinite suspension followed and despite requests to the LEA that the boy's name be deleted from the admission register (i.e. that he be expelled) this was not done. Boy Five enjoyed four months off school and took paid employment for most of the time. He returned to the school site four months later, just before the Easter holiday of 1976 and the day before his own statutory leaving date, bringing with him a bottle of beer. We presumed he had come to celebrate his victory over authority. Paradoxically, though able to take paid employment while still of compulsory school age, after compulsory school age there is no immediate need for these boys to work, as unemployment benefits may be enjoyed.

A number of points emerge as common to the five cases of which I write:

1 All five boys had passed beyond the school's control.
2 In every case the LEA rejected repeated requests by the headmaster and governors to have the boys' names deleted from the admission register.
3 In every case the LEA condoned indefinite suspension.
4 All five boys and their parents escaped any form of sanction.
5 In not one case did the LEA serve upon the parents a 'school attendance order' as required by Section 37(2) of the 1944 Act.

Many people have spoken out against the irregular device of the indefinite suspension. I have always maintained that to secure good discipline I need but one thing. Either that a suspended pupil be returned to the school after a reasonable period of suspension (say 4, 6 or exceptionally, 8 weeks), or that he be expelled and his name deleted from the school's admission register. Mr E. J. Dorrell, General Secretary of the Headmasters' Association, has said, 'Indefinite suspension is quite unacceptable as a policy.' Barbara Bullivant, writing recently in the magazine *Where* says: 'Suspension

should surely be followed by a final solution, either with the pupil returning to school quickly, or some other alternative being worked out involving, in most cases, removal from the register of the school.' The Chairman of the Kent Education Committee, Mr A. Lawton, at a recent meeting with my own Chairman and Vice Chairman of Governors has declared that suspensions if agreed or supported by him would be for a limited period only and not indefinite. However following recent correspondence I am not yet optimistic that we have seen an end of the indefinite suspension in Kent.

Now that schools are dealing with children and with those who are no longer children—a sizeable proportion of whom are difficult to control—there are a number of suggestions I would like to make. First, until such time as the Education Act be rewritten, LEAs can give support to their teachers in three ways: (1) By vigorously implementing the law as it stands at present, using every legal opportunity that presents itself. Whilst education remains a matter of law in the final resort only legal action can ensure compliance with the law or the punishment of law breakers. (2) By acting rapidly against malefactors. All teachers know that acts of indiscipline must be dealt with quickly, and education officers can help by making same-day decisions. (3) By devoting resources to professional expertise designed to implement (1) and (2) rather than directing money towards 'retreat centres', 'sanctuaries' and the like. Secondly, that those who legislate, prepare a new Education Act to update Sections 36 and 37 of the 1944 Act. This should bring it into line with the changed circumstance brought about by compelling sixteen-year-olds to remain at school. The inadequacy of some parents makes the provision of Section 36 unrealistic. Indeed the concept of compulsory education perhaps ought to be questioned. When in California I came across a school district publication which said, 'Students shall be held responsible for their own behaviour. While education is a right of American youth, it is not an absolute right. Our courts speak of education as a limited right or privilege; that is, should a student fail to perform those duties required of him upon attendance in public schools, he may then be denied his right to attend a public school.' I learnt from conversations I had whilst in the United

States, that employers look sideways at youngsters who fail to complete public school and that this alone acts as a considerable incentive to conform. Even so there are those who will not conform, but at least they know the price they will be paying. In England and Wales it is the school which counts the cost, and the decent majority of its pupils who pay the price.

Comprehensive inadequacies

STEPHEN WOODLEY

The secondary school teacher, unless he can find employment in the independent sector, or unless he really does see collectivisation as the main purpose of schooling, is liable to find himself compelled to live by a lie. If he is a young teacher, his chances of finding employment at all may depend on his appearing enthusiastic about the comprehensive principle; if an experienced teacher, he will evidently find promotion easier if he endorses these institutions. Nor will the good subject-teacher simply be able to take refuge in the academic integrity of his professional discipline, since it is precisely the incapacity of most comprehensives to offer the full range of subject-teaching at the full range of pupil ability that threatens the secondary curriculum and the examination system that has hitherto protected it against political directives.

As a secondary teacher I wish to assert two rights, such as the quinquennial financing of universities, guaranteed to the university teacher, including the Marxists. The first is the freedom to express my opinions on educational matters without thereby closing down my career, and the second is the freedom to teach a subject. In no way would I wish to disparage those of my fellow teachers working willynilly in comprehensives; as in a previous generation there were good teachers uneasy about the 11 plus, so now there are thousands of teachers who maintain the dignity of personal commitment to their pupils whilst not believing in the new system.

What the teachers really think was strikingly clear from *The Times Educational Supplement*/NOP Survey at the time of the last General Election.[1] Asked whether they agreed with the elimination of grammar schools, 70 per cent of the sample (of 1,173) said they did not, with only 55 per cent of the Labour voters and 16 per cent of the Liberals positively favouring this measure. By type of institution, only 26 per cent of the secondary and 18 per cent of the primary teachers favoured Labour's fundamentalist policies. As John Gretton's commentary observes, 'It really is a massive vote, by all sectors of the profession, against one of the principal trends of educational policy over the last ten years.' He added that it should worry a union like the National Union of Teachers (owing its financial and numerical strength to the primary sector) that its members' and its Executive's attitudes evidently 'point in different directions'.

Consider the situation of one representative of that 67 per cent of secondary teachers who declared themselves positively against the elimination of grammar schools. This teacher is interviewed for a senior post in a school shortly to be reorganised from a grammar school of 700, into a comprehensive of 1,000. The education officer wants to know how he feels such a school should adapt to new conditions, its staff acquire techniques for dealing with less able children, its thinking move away from GCE or university preparation. Is he to reply with the velleities of the Progressive Establishment ('this will be an exciting venture for everyone, and at no stage need the special needs of the more able be sacrificed'), or is he to express a syllable of his fears that to change from selective 700 to comprehensive 1,000 diminishes the academic and cultural opportunities of relatively able children in that area for the foreseeable future? If the latter, he will blandly be told he has 'an outmoded concept of sixth-form viability' (a shabby phrase), and he will be written off as a mere Black Paperite by an officer who continues his own way up through the hierarchy of a reorganising Conservative authority. Experience demonstrates what analysis suggests: the system is bound to facilitate the promotion of a certain kind of socialist and to impede everyone else. Nor, if there is an imbalance of view in the educational bureaucracy, need this be surprising; by and large the teachers most satisfied with the schools they were serving were the least likely to move into educational administration in the 1960s. As for the haste with which many Conservative authorities abandoned their grammar schools in those years, that can readily be explained by the uncertain sound of Sir Edward Boyle's trumpet and by the dependence every elected councillor has on the views of the professionals, unless he himself happens to be expert in the same field.

Nothing is clearer than that the comprehensive movement was the war—of that section of the middle class which designated itself progressive—on the rest. Moreover, the rapid growth of public expenditure on education created a new elite (of privilege if not always of responsibility) that could in general afford the luxury of pursuing absolute ends because it enjoyed secure access to public subsidy. Change could never have been so swift but for Robbins, not only because reorganisation assumes that the country will if necessary be rich enough to bail out a lethargic secondary sector by emulating the American pattern of awarding some 30,000 Ph.Ds a year, but also because Robbins meant that a generation of young academics who in another time would have been grateful for the allocation of some sixth-form teaching in a decent grammar school were whirled upstairs into university lectureships. Hence the strange spectacle we have in Canterbury, where the most militant demands for rapid reorganisation tend to come from people who are busy acquiring for themselves security of tenure in the most selective sector of education possible.

Such pharisaism calls in question the morality of what one might otherwise see as the rigorously Christian viewpoint that comprehensives are necessary because only they will bring the best-qualified teachers to the most disadvantaged pupils. When Mr Ernest Armstrong was Labour's Minister of State for Education he told a reporter: 'I don't think teachers should be allowed to choose whom they teach. Someone has to teach less able children and the ones who behave badly.'[2] There is a Mother Teresa logic lurking here—though a more secular mind might call it direction of labour—which I commend to those eleven members of the University of Kent Social Sciences Faculty who stood for Labour (naturally, no other team appeared on their programme) in the 1976 District Elections. I would also commend to these elevated egalitarians the example of a Poor Parson who preceded them to Canterbury:

'That first he wroghte, and afterward he taughte.'

For, just as the tripartite system maintained its elite groups, like scholarship teachers, so the comprehensive movement has its elites and their most prominent feature is that generally they are not in the schools at all. The familiar names are all outsiders: Professors Simon and Peston; Tyrell Burgess and Brian Jackson; and so on. That representative Penguin Special, *Education for Democracy*, had strong views on secondary education and, sure enough, 21 of its 22 contributors weren't in secondary education. The fact is that just as the enlarged schools have notoriously produced a non-teaching, or mini-teaching hierarchy within themselves, so reorganisation has extended the power of the bureaucrat, the adviser, the public communicator—the last-named particularly if he lives in London. There are indeed education administrators who interpret their role differently, but this cannot disguise the fact that the comprehensive system involves a fundamental shift of power to the bureaucracy. Schools can only be equalised and attainments made more uniform if the bureaucracy is empowered to zone, to bus, to allocate children according to abstractions like 'balanced intake' or 'social need'. The power of State monopoly can then be used to bully parents or intimidate teachers into silence.

One might wish to attribute these developments to well-meaning idealism, but a study of Professor Maurice Kogan's *The Politics of Education* can hardly be reassuring to anyone on the receiving rather than the profitable end of Mr Crosland's circular, 10/65.

Kogan's book makes clear the primacy of political objectives in reorganisation; he calls 10/65 'one of the most important Socialist actions of the Labour Government',[3] and Crosland says 'our belief in comprehensive reorganisation was a product of fundamental value-judgements'.[4] One of the most admired comprehensive schools has been Banbury, whose former Principal, Dr Harry Judge, is now director of the Oxford University department of education studies. It is some relief, therefore, to find him advocating—as indeed did earlier *Black Papers*—that there should be a re-examination of the possibility of diverse types of institutions existing from 14 and admitting 'It is idle to pretend that there survives . . . any powerful conviction that the present phase of comprehensive planning will bring any great educational improvement, or even be worth doing at all.'[5] Dr Judge can claim consistency for his views over a decade, but there is a hint of revisionism when the Editor of *The Times Educational Supplement*, Mr Stuart Maclure, confesses that 'the full, unadulterated comprehensive gospel is not held by many in the educational world and by few except ardent party ideologists anywhere.'[6] I shall offer a thanksgiving if they can help restore a tolerance of diversity in secondary education, but they'll find it hard work. I wonder, for a start, if Dr Judge can do something for that young graduate, of distinguished degree and good supporting record, who, in applying to us for a teaching appointment, said that he had been constrained to withdraw from a certain university's Education Department 'because I disagreed strongly with the methods of education being propounded, the lack of substance in the lectures' and the 'rather sneering attitude generally adopted by many of the staff towards traditional principles'. Whether Mr Maclure could recover for teaching that friend of mine, a man still in his twenties but of a breadth of experience more testing than the average sociology lecturer ever encounters, who described a first year of furious confrontations with such lecturers, a middle period of resentful silence, and a final stage of lauding the comprehensive system and plagiarising turgid Penguin Education Specials. He passed out of his college of educa-

tion with distinction, and has vowed never to go near teaching again.

What must we now urge? Three things, I believe: the value of discrete subject study; the importance of independent assessment in public examinations; a toleration of uncommon schools beyond 13 or 14. In fact, this is to ask the comprehensive movement to keep its promises, for it was the fundamental pledge of the reorganisers that no bright child would lose thereby. As lately as 1972 Mr Edward Short told a Canterbury audience that he himself would not believe in comprehensive schools if he were not confident they would educate the abler pupils as well as grammar schools had ever done. It is by now the conviction of a growing number of parents and teachers that this is not happening and in general will not happen.

At a recent parents' meeting in Maidstone about further reorganisation, attention was drawn to the restricted number of O-levels available in some comprehensives. Where it was not possible to take three full sciences at O-level pupils were handicapped in the competition for medical school places, for instance, and other opportunities in science were curtailed likewise. The reaction of Mr Eric Macfarlane, Principal of Queen Mary's Sixth Form College, to this viewpoint was that medical schools had no right to expect so much science anyway; and that of Mr Cyril Poster, Head of Sheppey School, was that minority subjects like German could perfectly well be left to 16. The anger and disbelief that was shown in response especially to the first of these replies showed the strength of parental feeling that academic subjects should remain fully available, and not be shuffled off. This particularly means that we must expose that current ideology which claims for comprehensives distinctive new curricula that will break down subject barriers as being humanly limiting, economically disastrous, and faithless.

The economic dimension is vital in itself. The UGC Report for 1974–5 drew attention to the number of students lacking basic skills in mathematics and modern languages, and the situation in the former can only get worse when one reads that the number of college of education entrants with an A-level in mathematics reached an all-time low in 1975. There must be a suspicion that those with useful qualifications are no longer attracted by the changed conditions of schools.

Outside higher education, the Director General of the Engineering Employers' Federation has called attention[7] to the dearth of sales and engineering staff able to speak other languages, as well as the new necessity of their training board offering remedial courses in literacy and mathematics to young people entering the industry. Similarly, it is hard to see how we shall produce engineers to maintain the CEGB when there will not be a graduate physics teacher per school if these are spread equally. The problem will be worse if 16–19 colleges increase, attracting the scarcer graduates. It may then become impossible to offer the proper curriculum from 11 to 16.

At this point, the seriousness of 16 plus examinations is evident, since they shape or reflect the curriculum of preceding years. Theoretically, a common system need not damage subject teaching nor need it mean a common exam, but one's confidence in the Schools Council's intentions is shaken by their talk of a continuum of ability and the need to be rid of the division of GCE and CSE. For these exams themselves cover only the upper sixty percentiles of ability, and a division made at point forty is neither more nor less justifiable than O-level. But in all this jobbery we shall have the support of the public if we insist that teachers should not act as both advocate and judge of their own pupils, except in limited areas. The upper grades at any rate should be assessed externally for not less than half the marks and more commonly for all of them.

There remains the alternative advocated by Lord Alexander of Potterhill and others on cost-efficiency grounds, vocally supported in some areas by the main FE union, NATFHE. This is the stripping of the post-16 education from the schools and the concentration of all 16–19 work in tertiary colleges. Academically, legislation for tertiary colleges would mean some important subjects not being taught at all before 16. If it were to happen it would kill secondary teaching as a career, and would be the most bitter of all blows to those grammar school teachers who were promised that all the best features of their school-work would be maintained in the comprehensives.

As we are pushed from one new scheme to the next, children suffer from these ill-prepared plans, and teachers who care about their subjects can only despair.

NOTES

1 'Teachers in the British General Election of October 1974' (Times Newspapers Ltd).
2 *The Times Educational Supplement*, 4 April 1975.
3 *The Politics of Education*, Ed. Kogan, Penguin, p. 16.
4 *ibid*. p. 190.
5 *The Times Educational Supplement*, 2 May 1975.
6 *The Times Educational Supplement*, 18 April 1975.
7 *The Times*, 29 June 1976.

An alternative curriculum

GEOFFREY BANTOCK

For nearly twenty years now I have been arguing that the crisis in our secondary education is cultural and cannot be met by the organisational device of the comprehensive school. Indeed, comprehensivisation with its aspirations towards a common curriculum simply exacerbates a situation which was already apparent in the ideological bankruptcy of the secondary modern school, encouraged as it was by its new secondary status to disguise its uncertainties of aim and purpose by aping the grammar schools. Since then, equality of concern—which is acceptable—has been interpreted as requiring similarity or sameness of provision—which is not. The outcome has been a growing dissatisfaction with comprehensive education on the part of the public in general, and desperate curricular and organisational devices within the institutions—'integration' of subject-matter to provide 'relevance' and non-streaming are the most obvious ones—to produce at least an appearance of adequacy. The problem is, of course, world wide; and an Australian critic, A. A. Phillips, has expressed the resulting dilemma in simple but devastating terms: 'The new type [of secondary school pupil] is being allowed to erode the standards of our elite education, and simultaneously to suffer a type of education not suited to his needs.'

I shall not here repeat the analysis, which I have given in numerous other places, of how and why this situation has been allowed to develop. What are now needed are positive suggestions for a more adequate educational experience for that section of the school population which even in the relaxed academic circumstances prevailing in many of our comprehensives today is still clearly not benefiting. For some time[1] now I have been advocating what I have termed a theory of popular education, in which I have attempted, in the light of a deep analysis of our present-day culture and of its putative suitability for the various intellectual levels in our community, to suggest alternative offerings for those who cannot cope with the pre-eminently cognitively oriented curriculum of our secondary schools. My suggestions have attracted some attention—much of it predictably hostile. I want here to expound briefly what these suggestions are, together with an indication of the reasoning behind them. Then I wish to deal with some of the criticisms that have been made, and thus take the argument a stage further. For clearly, the learning experiences we offer our children in the schools are fundamental to the whole business of education; if they prove unacceptable, the enterprise must inevitably fail.

My proposals arise out of an awareness of the tensions which exist between action and consciousness in human affairs. Human beings inhabit a symbolic world, a world capable of being conceptualised. Thus, between a stimulus and a human response, thought, which results from an ability to handle such concepts, to work out their interrelationships, and to draw on the resources of memory, interposes an awareness, a consciousness of the situation which can make human reaction one of reason, not simply of instinct. Not all human behaviour is thus thought out; much of it is but some of it is the result of habit; and the area subject to reason has, with the expansion of human knowledge, vastly increased with the centuries. (A fictional treatment of what I have in mind will be found in Shakespeare's *Hamlet*; the popularity of that play points to the universality of the problem.)

But various people's capacity for reasoning differs immensely and may be intimately bound up with the actuality of the situation under review. As William Blake put it, 'a fool sees not the same tree that a wise man sees'; and if such differences exist even in direct contact—and I do not see how they can be denied—various recording devices men have invented introduce possibilities of further abstraction which make the differences even more apparent. Writing, for instance, permits the codification and storing of information for future deployment which immensely complicates the direct act of perception and exacerbates the differences between novices and initiates. It also greatly complicates the task of initiation—the less intelligent get left further and further behind.

In essence we have here the progress of Western civilisation and therefore of Western education which undertakes the task of initiation. The diffusion of literacy would appear to have opened the door to the accumulated knowledge of the ages, which is now so complex as to depend on written or printed codification for its preservation; but mere access does not guarantee assimilation. In general, it is safe to assume that the higher the degree of abstraction, the fewer are the people who can handle such abstractions with any confidence. (By 'degree of abstraction', I mean the degree to which we depart from the phenomenal world in actual or symbolic form; few people have any difficulty in *conceiving* of *concrete* actualities in their absence.) This difference in ability has nothing *necessarily* to do with social class, except in so far as the classes differ in their degree of exposure to conceptual usage, a fact which may in part explain the comparative conceptual impoverishment of the working-class child; but similar impoverishment can easily be identified in other classes: more than exposure is necessary.

Yet, of course, our academic education is geared precisely to the transmission of a set of conceptual schemes through which we come to understand the various 'subjects' of the curriculum—that curriculum which many of the advocates of comprehensive education insist should be common to all: in essence, the grammar school curriculum. The emphasis—very rightly for those who can cope—is on knowledge, on that human symbolic world which interposes itself between man and his activity and which provides him with some of the characteristic tools of his rationality, in its many and varied guises.

This does not mean that rationality is only for some; but it does mean that some are more restricted than others in the areas within which they can act rationally; and even within these areas, the methods we use to induce that consciousness, which is the essential concomitant of rationality, may well differ from those we employ with children who show a greater aptitude for handling the higher level abstractions. To put the matter in Piagetian terms, many children may not be able to get beyond the level of concrete operations, while others may progress quite easily into that of formal operations.

It is because I believe this truly to diagnose our educational situation—and it could, I believe, be demonstrated in every comprehensive school in the land—that I have suggested that to begin with, we approach the education of our lowest achieving children through a new content and by different methods. To put it in its broadest terms, I suggest that we place a greater emphasis on action than on reflection and that such powers of reflection as these low academic achievers are capable of should spring out of such activity; and that, as a vital source of such action greater attention should be paid to the affective sides of their natures. Now to translate these broad generalities into concrete terms.

I assume that basic literacy and numeracy have been acquired through carefully structured and disciplined learning in the primary school (a rash assumption, indeed, but perhaps a trifle more acceptable in the aftermath of Dr Neville Bennett's research, and the William Tyndale imbroglio), and that opportunities for suitable reading will always be sought at secondary level. The question now arises as to whether further introduction to the humanities should be made through the conventional subjects—English, history, geography, social studies and the like, with their dependence on literacy and the book—or whether some new approach, based on a more primitive kinaesthetic potential would not provide a better introduction to the level of consciousness of which these children are capable. It is not without significance that the various human arts (apart from literature, which is a comparatively late arrival) depend on articulation through gestures—dance, drama, ritual, music, painting, sculpture and crafts of many kinds as well as aspects of what is termed physical education. It is as though man's basic way of absorbing his world is through disciplined action and the physical exploration of the space within which he moves. Such movements are not instinctual—human responses are essentially learned responses, and talk of 'spontaneity' is out of place. Discipline, therefore, is involved, and a level of consciousness which needs to come to terms with important aspects of the reality of the world—but in its concrete manifestations. Furthermore, though practically no human activities can be categorised as exclusively cognitive or emotional, clearly the activities I have in mind contribute more to emotional than to cognitive education—at least they belong to the affective orientation of the cognitive-affective continuum. Work with subnormal children has already shown the benefits to be gained from this sort of emphasis;[2] and the world of the mongol can be regarded as an intensified form of the world of intellectual dullness to which many of the reluctant learners of our schools belong.

So disciplined movement, of the sort fostered in this country by Rudolf Laban (who urged that 'Dance is not to relieve feelings, it is not self-expression; dance is no longer spontaneous gestures but deliberate acts') forms, in a variety of artistic and craft guises, the basis of an education intended to enable the less intellectually endowed child to move with confidence amidst the concrete actualities of his civilisation. Drama, of course, brings in speech and the niceties of oral communication. Furthermore, many of these activities are social in character and afford opportunities for communal participation.

Another area to which much greater attention should be paid in schools is constituted by those characteristic twentieth-century art forms—film, television, radio. Film making and editing, and photography, enable children to develop an iconographic awareness which can, if properly handled, make them more critically aware of the possibilities of the media they are much more likely to encounter in their daily lives than that of print.[3] It is important that these visual and aural media should be treated for their expressive qualities and not simply as teaching aids. In this way something may be done to counteract aspects of popular culture when material is transmitted which is totally inadequate to the quality and complexity of the emotional life of its receivers.

All this would take up about three-fifths of the time. For the rest, domestic and other aspects of technical education should be offered to both boys and girls. In this way, understanding can be built up in relation to the actualities of social and technical life—the preparation of food, simple hygiene, some of the technical demands implicit in running a home and so on.

This, in brief summary, and without the supporting arguments possible in fuller expositions (which the interested reader is strongly advised to consult), constitutes the broad outlines of the scheme. The criticisms it has provoked can be roughly categorised into three groups—philosophical, social and political, and what might be broadly termed practical. Clearly, to some extent the categories overlap, but some such sorting out enables me to concentrate on answering those points which are likely to be of most interest to the general reader.

The more technical, philosophical objections can be dealt with quite rapidly as in most cases they stem from an insufficiently exact reading of my article in *The Times Educational Supplement*. Thus I have been accused of holding an expressionist theory of art, a charge against which my quotation from Laban, with its rejection of dance as the relief of feelings and its emphasis on

'deliberate acts', dance essentially as a shaping and a making, should have protected me. I see these activities as disciplines, not simply as outpourings or releases; I am concerned with education, not therapy. Then, astonishingly, I am accused of perpetuating an affective/cognitive dichotomy, as if I believed that disciplines could be allocated exclusively to one or the other category. I have made it abundantly clear in a number of places that I accept no such dichotomy; and within the articles concerned I state specifically that 'my ultimate aim' constitutes an 'approach to consciousness and mind (. . . it is a fundamental error not to see that, as the arts develop, they inevitably come to involve knowledge and understanding)'; it could hardly be more explicit.

A more interesting point, and one of more general interest, urges that it is a mistake to think that less able children will necessarily find the disciplines of movement less exacting than disciplines of other kinds:

> . . . the discipline of *composing*, of wrestling with motifs, contrasts . . . is just as rigorous and demanding in dance . . . as in any other art. And the ability of intellectually less able children . . . to imagine, to formulate and to structure, is hardly likely to be less limited than in other fields.[4]

Of course such children will produce work in the various arts and crafts which is likely to be of limited value; and I see no reason to doubt that intellectually able children will, in general, shine also in artistic subjects. But the important point is that intellectually limited children can, in general, make some sort of a shot at the affectively oriented subjects whereas they are totally lost, in the majority of cases, where the more cognitively oriented subjects are concerned. We all have bodies, though some are inevitably clumsier in their movements than others; the ungainly will produce less refined results than their more graceful compeers. But comparable cognitive demands will produce no results whatsoever from the intellectually dull.

Some, of course, would deny this last point and urge that a denial of common cognitive opportunities to all children cannot be justified, on the grounds that the potential of such children can never be gauged with sufficient accuracy as to justify their allocation, at a comparatively early age, to an alternative educational diet. We now begin to become involved in arguments with social and political overtones.

Are there, then, rational grounds for believing that some children are constitutionally incapable of following an intellectually demanding curriculum? Clearly one critic thinks not: he describes such a view as 'not a rational belief; it is rather an article of faith'.[5]

Let me first freely admit that such a contention of incapacity could not be *proved*; indeed, to expect proof would be irrational, for it is clearly not reasonable to expect man to do what by nature he is incapable of doing, that is to predict, infallibly, the future. It is only reasonable to expect men to proceed on grounds which can be defended rationally as appertaining to the nature of the case in hand.

Now, when a child enters a secondary school of any type, comprehensive or other, inevitably a decision has to be taken as to what he is to learn there. The fact that in many comprehensive schools this question is not formally asked—because it is the set policy of the school that all children shall follow a common curriculum—does not mean that a decision has not in fact been taken. (There is somehow a belief that not to allocate children to different learning programmes obviates the need for justification. But not to allocate involves just as much of a decision requiring justification as does allocation. *All* educational decisions concerning curricular choices involve value judgements and need therefore to be capable of rational justification. The fact that the decision is allowed to go by default is simply indicative of our current social idiosyncrasies.)

It is idiotic to argue that there is no evidence available to help those who would be responsible for allocating children to the sort of curriculum I am suggesting. There are the results of intelligence and achievement tests, reports from the primary schools, knowledge about home background and parental support, opportunities for close consultation with previous teachers. After all, any child of secondary school age has already undergone a five-year period during which diagnosis can be carried out; one could only wish that all our social decisions could be taken with such a weight of evidence available.

I have already admitted that such evidence can never be totally definitive, and would freely grant that occasional errors will almost inevitably be made. But this is always true of any academic or social decision which is ever made. Human beings are not gods, and they must, as I have urged, learn to operate within the restrictions which the fallibility of human capacity for prediction necessarily imposes. In the light of the sort of evidence which I have listed above, it is perfectly reasonable to predict that some children, at least, will be unable to cope with an intellectually demanding curriculum. We are not proceeding irrationally or on the basis of what our critic implies is 'faith'; we are proceeding responsibly, on the basis of the best evidence available. Indeed, it would be perfectly reasonable to throw the onus of decision-making onto our critic by asking him on what grounds, in the face of the available evidence, he would argue that certain specific children show any potential whatsoever for the sort of curriculum he has in mind. As the husband of someone who has taught remedial reading in a state primary school for many years I would be delighted to attend and listen to discussions about the potential of specific children in the light of experience of such children gathered over a long period of time. I know, too, that my wife would readily welcome those suggestions for alternative methods which in the eyes of our critic would appear to offer the promise of turning her geese into swans.

'Ah! that's it', I can hear other critics exclaim—'geese' and 'swans'; I am labelling some children as inferior. Actually, geese, to anyone who has looked at them properly, are fine, handsome birds; and swans can be ill-natured beasts. But it so happens that, however much one may wish nature had arranged things differently, geese just aren't swans. There is an indication of this sort of criticism in the accusation that my aim is simply 'to keep the peasants happy'. There is not, I think, anything inherently wicked in the attempt to make people happy; but, in fact, the implications behind 'peasants' should not be allowed to stand. Indeed, one very important consideration that reconciles me to the likelihood of error in some small degree in the matter of allocation arises from the nature of the alternative curriculum I am offering. It seems to me to afford two sorts of opportunity. There are, in the first place, possible occupational opportunities. One of the major practical objections which has been urged against my scheme is that by adopting it we shall be spoiling the occupational opportunities of the children concerned, cutting them off from the sort of prestige job which requires the type of certification which is geared to the conventional curriculum.

But what in fact at present faces the sort of child I have defined here? Not indeed a prestige job but repetitive work in a factory of that soul-destroying type which constitutes one of the great dilemmas of our technological civilisation. On the other hand, what I would offer them certainly has its occupational possibilities. The increase in leisure and the proliferation of popular art forms which the revolution in communications of our times has led to is engendering new occupations of various types. Characteristic of these new occupations are the emotional manifestations which it is the job of my curriculum to afford some training in—and some protection against the vulgarity (and worse) fostered by these manifestations is in any case sorely needed. If we offer the sort of curriculum I am suggesting to our low achievers, it is perfectly reasonable to hope that some at least will mature in a way which the present cognitive emphasis of the curriculum has signally failed to achieve. In other words, I am suggesting that opportunities will be afforded—in the sphere of communications, for instance—which at present don't exist for these children. I am not so romantic as to think that all or even many will be able to seize these opportunities; but they certainly won't—they couldn't—be worse off than they are at the moment.

Then there are other opportunities which stem from the quality of the material itself. This is not one of those life-adjustment programmes with its exclusive emphasis on the banalities of daily life (I shall say more about these in a moment); it is not an education for helots—or peasants, for that matter. To be acceptable to the conscience of the age it must contain a strong element which is genuinely liberalising—and this is precisely what it does. It can open up many of the riches of European civilisation, for it exploits, for instance, many of the same devices that the medieval church employed in its attempt to transmit its message to the people. (It is interesting to note that many of these popular devices—the paintings, the sculptures, the music etc.—have gradually down the ages become the preserves of the elite. Why? A good remedial teacher can get her charges absorbed and delighted by reproductions of some of the great masterpieces of the past: they love the colours, the clothes and—an actual comment—the sense of peace in a Claude landscape.) In all these respects it shows no inherent inferiority to the more conventional, cognitively based curriculum. It is simply founded on different and, in some respects, more fundamental principles. Properly handled it involves discipline and structure to exactly the same extent as the cognitive approach.

Furthermore it challenges the adequacy of other alternative programmes. During the last few years the importance of cultural factors has at last been belatedly recognised. The recognition, however, has proceeded on class divisive lines. Work on class speech differentiations stemming from the pioneer work of Professor Basil Bernstein has led to the appreciation that different elements of our school population employ somewhat different linguistic codes; and in a situation where language plays so vital a part an explanation has been suggested for the persistent under-achievement which seems to characterise working-class children in so many countries, and for the comparative failure of so many compensatory programmes. A politically inspired concerted effort has been made to denigrate the cognitive curriculum on the grounds that it represents the symbolic knowledge system by which the middle classes maintain their social hegemony and, at the same time, to quote *The Times Educational Supplement*, 'to keep the poor in their place'. In its place the viability of an alternative culture, equally 'valid' and worthwhile, is insisted on—that of the working classes.

The argument is sustained, of course, by subtly shifting the sense of the word 'culture'. Anthropologists use it to refer to the total pattern of a society's life; in this article it has been used in a restricted, evaluative sense relevant to an educational debate for, as I have stated above, curricular decisions always involve value decisions. In the first sense, the working classes clearly have a culture, one which in a number of ways—in methods of child rearing, for instance—differs from that of the middle classes. But in the qualitative sense there is no evidence that they possess one sufficiently differentiated from that of the middle classes to provide adequate material for an alternative school curriculum. Indeed, as the pre-industrial folk have developed into the modern urban working classes, there is evidence of specific decline and atrophy in a number of fields. Industrial folk song of the nineteenth century was inferior to that of its rural forbears; and Martha Vicinus in her recent book *The Industrial Muse* has charted the decline of street ballads and broadsheets, working-class poetry and fiction, dialect literature and the rest during the nineteenth century, and its final demise under the impact of mass entertainment: 'In the twentieth century it is no longer possible to speak of a separate working-class literature.' Industrialisation has killed the very real culture of the folk in pre-industrial times.

All this comes through very clearly in the sort of specific recommendations that working-class apologists make concerning relevant areas of cultural interest. What educational potential is there to be found in horse and dog racing, boxing, pigeon fancying, variety and pop, betting shop and bingo session?[6] What an insult to the potential of even our backward children are these suggestions by Mr Brian Jackson:

> Spend any time in a decaying back street, and you'll see how important television or football pools are. Or chalking on walls. Or pulling a motor bike to pieces. Or a group of girls dolling up each other's hair. Why isn't the education there, putting on children's chalking competitions, building runnable cars out of junk, dressmaking, street theatre, 'holiday at home' weeks.

Only dressmaking—and possibly street theatre, though one would want to know what is involved—offer any potential here. Strenuous attempts, however, are being made to represent 'the vernacular culture of the streets' as a viable alternative to the culture of the school. The feasibility of comparing cultures is raised. Referring to 'high culture' two other critics point out that 'The use of the qualifier "high" is a valuation: the culture in question is being rated higher than others', and ask 'Are we entitled to make such a valuation?'[7]

The answer, of course, is a categorical 'yes', though justification in detail would require much more space than is available. I can, however, indicate the terms on which such justification can proceed. Clearly, judgments about cultures, even in their restricted sense, can only emerge as the result of a vast series of particular judgments about specifics. Thus, to give an example, love lyrics from pop songs—'pop' is noted above as one of the areas characterising working-class culture, which is why I have chosen the example—can be compared with a series of love poems by a representative selection of received poets. The results could be judged in terms of their adequacy to the human experience of love, whether the images they transmit are simply stereotyped or extend one's awareness of the nature of love, their use of language and so forth. The question as to whether some readers could benefit from the more profound treatments is irrelevant to the issue at stake—we are concerned to assess the relative merits of the cultural artefacts, not to judge the psychological competence of the audience: the two matters are quite distinct.

In this way, through the careful, detailed analysis of specific contents in numerous fields the sceptical, provided they approach the matter with reasonable, open minds—willing to argue the matter in a spirit of free inquiry—can be convinced. But of course, behind much of current emphasis on cultural relativism there are tendentious political objectives, dogmatic egalitarian beliefs which no amount of rational discussion can alter. (It is interesting to note that what might be referred to as the 'old left' are at least as critical of 'relativist sociologists' as I am. Thus, Mrs Joan Simon in the journal of which her husband is the editor, *Forum*, in an article entitled ' "New Direction" Sociology and Comprehensive Schooling' accuses these 'new direction' sociologists of 'providing a formula for actual cultural deprivation of the working class'.[8] It is true that Mrs Simon and I would disagree on the remedy for this situation—she repeats, elsewhere in her article, the old charge about my desire to keep ' "the folk" happy at their own level'. But the sort of nonsense I have quoted above well sustains her belief that the effect of the relativist approach would indeed serve to deprive low achieving children (whether working class or not) of opportunities for cultural enrichment.)

'Enrichment', indeed, is the key word. For

many of these criticisms stem from a philistine inability to assess the potential of what I am offering. It would be a thousand pities, now that it is being realised, in some degree, that the crisis is cultural—a significant advance beyond the naivety of those who for so long have seen the dilemmas of secondary education in exclusively organisational terms—if the *quality* of any alternative offering were not the prior consideration; if a sort of perverted pastoralism, as foolish in its day as the pretence of the eighteenth-century French court to find a satisfactory, alternative way of life in the habits and behaviour of milkmaids and rustics, were to induce us to admit the claims of the culture of our present day urban proletariat as providing a satisfactory alternative to the cognitively oriented curriculum.

Clearly these suggestions are offered for debate in what has become a major twentieth-century problem—how do we cope with something new in the history of mankind, a total school population. I lack the arrogance of the comprehensivists, who would impose their schemes on everybody by law; and I shall be satisfied if in a few schools a few teachers are stimulated to look to their procedures, to question their current engagement, to test the validity of some of the suggestions I have made. The response from the theorists has been disappointing—some minor philosophical points which have usually stemmed from an imperfect reading of the words in front of them, and some predictable political hostility. But little attempt to assess the scheme at any fundamental level—at the level represented by, say, D. H. Lawrence's cry: 'For the mass of people, knowledge *must* be symbolical, mythical, dynamic'—has been made. For clearly, though there is much with which I would disagree in Lawrence's educational ideas, my analysis owes something to his influence, to his quite fundamental critique of our modern education.[9]

Indeed, no one has spotted the great practical question mark which hangs over the whole endeavour. For even if acceptable, what I have to offer will stand or fall ultimately by the quality of the teachers who will have to put it into operation. Here I have wavered between optimism and pessimism. I am optimistic because I believe that there is a sizable minority of teachers who would themselves welcome a change of orientation; there are many teachers in our schools today who are seeking to transmit a culture in which they don't really believe, and which they themselves, though they may have acquired a limited technical competence in the fields in which they teach, have failed to internalise in any significant way. We should face up to the implications of the fact that their culture is as fully oriented to the popular media as to that based on literacy and the book; critical analyses of these other media might offer to them a more satisfying cultural experience, with corresponding improvement in their commitment to the educational enterprise.

But it is the *quality* of that commitment which would then be in question. As I have said elsewhere, 'My fear is that in seeking the implementation of what I am recommending I may simply be opening the floodgates to an avalanche of exploitable pop instead of the training (slow but possible) in affective discrimination I intend.' Or again, 'progressive' fears of interference with children's spontaneous likings will inhibit teachers from playing the very positive role in introducing children to material of quality which will be necessary. For of course these children above all will have little to offer 'creatively', as it were, out of their meagre and restricted experience; they will need to be told stories, mime characters created by others, look at pictures, use myths and legends to which they have been introduced as a basis for their dramatic work, examine the craft work of others. And where are the teachers with the necessary experience, the interest and the knowledge to perform these very positive functions? The capacity for refined emotional discrimination is as rare as high cognitive ability.

To say this is simply to stress once more that we live in an imperfect world, and that there are no *solutions* to problems of the magnitude of those which I have been dealing with in this article. All one can do is to make one's depositions and honestly and squarely face the pitfalls; by exposing the latter, indeed, one may in some appreciable degree contribute to their avoidance. Certainly, the expression of the fear serves to highlight my purpose, which is education and not recreation, discipline and not indulgence. What I can point to is that although as a whole what I am suggesting has not been tried, various of the elements do of course already appear in the schools.

Music, art and craft, and drama are common-place; slowly but increasingly attention is being paid to movement and to the new expressive media of television and film. As yet there is no tradition of criticism and discrimination in many of these fields to serve as guidelines, as exists, for instance, in that of literature. But one must maintain some small faith in the capacity of human beings to seek the necessary discernment, once their attention has been focused on the need. That ghastly mistakes will occur is simply to demonstrate that they are, after all, human.

NOTES

1 First suggested in my *Education in an Industrial Society* (Faber 1963, 2nd edn 1973); then in 'Towards a Theory of Popular Education' (*The Times Educational Supplement*, 12 and 19 March 1971, reprinted in *The Curriculum* Ed. R. Hooper, Open University Press, 1971), and further elaborated in 'The Reluctant Learner' in *Melbourne Studies in Education 1972* Ed.

R. J. W. Selleck, Melbourne University Press, 1972.

2 Cf. P. Tuckwell, 'The Theatre of the Subnormal' *(New Society* 14 January 1971).

3 The latest study of the National Children's Bureau's development project reveals that 27 per cent of 15,000 16-year-olds studied, never, or hardly ever, read a book on their own. 65 per cent often watched TV. (*The Times* report, 13 September 1976.)

4 H. B. Redfern: ' "Movement" and Professor Bantock's Theory of Popular Education', *Gazette* no. 20, Autumn 1975, University of Manchester School of Education, p. 40.

5 Cf. J. P. White: *Towards a Compulsory Curriculum*, Routledge & Kegan Paul.

6 Cf. C. MacInnes in *The Times Educational Supplement*, 5 October 1973.

7 J. Reynolds and M. Skilbeck: *Culture and the Classroom*, p. 71.

8 *Forum*, Autumn 1974, p. 12.

9 Cf. my chapter on D. H. Lawrence in *Freedom and Authority in Education*, Faber.

Evolution by choice

STUART SEXTON

Let's try to sketch out a new system for secondary education. Obviously we get rid of the 1976 Education Act for a start. We remove all other political constraints and directions which seek to distort the pattern of *educational* supply and demand. We have to assume that the politicians keep their fingers out of it, apart from laying down the framework within which variety and diversity can abound in accordance with the aspirations and abilities of the children.

As part of that framework we must have minimum standards and a minimum curriculum.

Variety and diversity do not mean a free-for-all where educational standards are forgotten in a desire to be different. Also, one expects an effective and independent Inspectorate for *all* schools, monitoring those standards, advising and assisting, but never dictating.

Choice of school

Our concern is that *all* children should find the right education; it is not a question of concentrating on the top 20 per cent and neglecting the rest, neither is it the equally stupid but current mistake of attempting to look after the 70 or 80 per cent majority to the detriment of the most able. Nevertheless, my concern in this paper is to indicate the evolution of the comprehensive and other non-selective schools. We may assume that in our new-found freedom, the remaining grammar schools will be free to prosper, and the ex-direct-grant schools reinstated and expanded, so that between them all there will be a network of highly academic schools throughout the country to which any child, regardless of parental income, would be free to apply, and if suitable, would be accepted. However, even this special mention of the highly academic schools is strictly speaking unnecessary, because, as will be seen, they will all be just good schools to which any parent may apply. The parent should be able to apply to *any* secondary school; there should be no zones, no catchment areas. Certainly such applications could be processed through the local education authority so that the parent need not apply separately to each school; but if so used, the Town Hall should be little more than a post office, consolidating the lists, passing them on to the schools. The bureaucracy would certainly not 'allocate' children to schools; how dreadfully impersonal that expression is!

Choice of child

Thus for a start, absolute freedom of choice of application. If the school is undersubscribed, then it is also absolute freedom of choice of school—you get the place you want. If on the other hand the school is oversubscribed then some form of selection remains to be done, but this time selection on educational criteria, not on where you happen to live. The governors and head of the school would choose from the list of applications those children most suitable on ability and aptitude for that particular school. Obviously primary school records, interviews, and all available information would be necessary, and for a school specialising in highly academic work there may well be a formal examination as well. Indeed for specialist schools whether academic, linguistic, scientific, for music, for dancing, or for some such particular aptitude, selection will always be necessary whether or not the school is over-subscribed.

Special aptitude

For example, in some schools strong mathematics departments have developed. This is a particularly apposite example because good mathematics teachers are scarce and any child with a particular aptitude for mathematics should be encouraged to enter a school where the mathematics teaching is strong. Whereas at present a cross-section of children from the immediate neighbourhood will go to that school under the comprehensive allocation system, among whom a few may be especially bright at mathematics, under free choice parents with 'mathematics' children will seek out schools where mathematics is prominent, and conversely, such schools, in interviewing their applicants, will be looking for mathematics children in particular. It is a two-way exercise: the parent has a vested interest in seeing that his child's specialisation is met, the school, in building up still more its excellent traditions. In this example the child need not be 11 years old, he may well be 12 or 13 before the specialisation really develops.

Examples of music, or dancing, or singing are obvious. We have come to expect special selection for musical or dancing skills, both on the part of the parent and on the part of the school. Quite simply, this can be extended to other specialisations or, if specialisation is too strong a word, to a greater emphasis in one direction rather than in another. Furthermore, we need not limit ourselves to academic specialisation; just as some seek out a Roman Catholic education, or a girls only school, so all should be able to seek out differences in ethos, in discipline, Christian teaching, in sporting prowess or whatever.

Evolution of the schools

What I have described is not particularly novel: it merely extends admissions policy to the governors and heads of all schools, including the County Schools. It will be seen that the interplay of 'choice of school' by the parent on the one hand, and 'choice of child' by the school on the other, with the elimination of bureaucratic direction between them, will result over a period of time in a flexible response by the schools to the needs of the children and the preference of their parents. The parents will be 'voting with their feet' and schools will have to respond, or have no pupils.

This evolution is greatly helped by the present

situation of falling numbers. It means that over the next few years, fewer secondary school places will be needed, but the places to decrease should be those the parents reject, not the ones the bureaucrats find it administratively most convenient to close.

Variety of school

In the towns, where the child population is sufficient to support many secondary schools, perhaps twenty all within easy reach of home, instead of having twenty theoretically equal, mixed comprehensive schools, all as good (or as bad) as each other, those twenty comprehensives could and would evolve differently according to different parental demand. Some would be single-sex, others mixed; some denominational, others secular; some would be more academic, some more technical, some with a tradition of classics, others of science; some with a notable music department, others with a reputation in sport; and the parent could choose. Little Johnny would not be doing classics just because his neighbourhood comprehensive has a good classics master; he would be doing it because he, or his parents, sought out where such a good classics tradition could be found, which may, or may not, be the nearest school to home.

In rural areas the all-embracing comprehensive is still likely to be the norm, if for no other reason than the sheer practical impossibility of having more than one, or at the most two, secondary schools to serve a large area of sparse population. Under any system the country boy or girl is going to have far less choice of school simply because there can be only a few schools within reach of home, unless the child boards out, which may very well be necesary for certain specialisations such as music.

Flexible transfer

Having chosen and been accepted for a school place at the age of 11 or 12, or even 13, there must still be a flexible transfer system, and this is where the old tripartite 11 + system (or bipartite as it was in most cases) broke down in practice. This new system will not be bipartite or even tripartite, but multipartite. There will be many different schools and pupils must be able to transfer easily, even if they develop late. In practice only a few are

likely to need this facility, given that choice replaces direction in the first place, but nevertheless it should be there.

Devolution to the school

Hand in hand with the return of admissions policy to the schools, including the county schools, and thus a direct response to parental wishes, would be a devolution of the rest of the administration of the schools from the Town Hall to the Bursar or Secretary at the school itself. There is no reason why a maintained school should not be an independent unit just as in the private sector.

Vouchers

Just a word on vouchers. The use of a voucher, a piece of paper emphasising that each parent has the right to so many pounds' worth of education is not essential to the exercise of parental choice and need not be part of the scheme I have described. Nevertheless, it could well be very useful to the exercise of free choice and could be of great psychological value in emphasising to the parent that he has that choice. Such choice must always be modified, vouchers or not, by the school itself, especially if it is oversubscribed. Even vouchers cannot give absolute choice. Particularly in the early days of any voucher scheme, there must be sufficient choice available to start with, else when the voucher system failed to produce the choice expected, it would quickly fall into disrepute.

Towards a new freedom

After this new-found freedom has run for a school cycle, say seven years or so, there will begin to emerge schools, good schools, diverse in size, in organisation and in specialisation. The old school labels and the old battle of reorganisation, of grammar versus comprehensive, of petitioning and objecting, and all the rest, will seem like so many irrelevant childish squabbles. Once we give the parents the power, they won't let the politicians take it back.

The exercise of parental choice is the key. The very exercise of that choice, and the response to that choice, will produce the schools which the parents want and the children need. The comprehensives will evolve from the present mediocre sameness imposed by the bureaucracy towards the diversity demanded by the parents. They will be different, school to school, country to town, just as children are different. They will be good schools or they will close.

Someone once said 'trust the people'. Let us 'trust the parents'—to choose and to choose the best.

COMPREHENSIVE SCHOOLS

Questions

1 Why were comprehensives introduced so quickly without any research?

2 If it is claimed by their protagonists that comprehensive schools are doing so well, why not publish their examination results?

3 Mrs Shirley Williams now admits that big comprehensives were a mistake. Why not carry out proper research into other forms of comprehensives which may also be unsuccessful?

4 In the 1960s the comprehensive lobby argued that large comprehensives were necessary to provide a full range of subjects. If now we are to have smaller comprehensives will these schools provide a full range of subjects?

5 Is it true that able, working-class children leave earlier from comprehensives than from grammar schools?

6 In a sixth-form college system will not the 11–16 schools fail to recruit teachers of high academic ability?

7 Are there enough graduate teachers in physics, chemistry and maths to staff all comprehensives?

8 If a middle-class area has an excellent comprehensive and a working-class area a bad comprehensive, is this not socially divisive?

9 If mixed ability classes are more difficult to manage will not the average teacher fail with these methods?

10 How comprehensive are comprehensives?

3
Values

Background

Hannah Arendt, a German Jewess who fled from the Nazis to America, is best-known as a brilliant political theorist. Her attack on progressive education was published in *Between Past and Future* (1961) and is particularly relevant to the problem of adult authority. She argues that in the United States the fashion for child-centred education led to all the rules of sound human reason being thrust aside. The abdication of authority by parents and teachers is unnatural. The authority that tells the individual child what to do and what not to do comes to rest with the child group itself, and this produces a situation in which the adult stands helpless before the individual child and out of contact with him. He can only tell him to do what he likes and then prevent the worst from happening. The real and normal relations between children and adults are thus broken off:

> . . . by being emancipated from the authority of adults the child has not been freed but has been subjected to a much more terrifying and truly tyrannical authority, the tyranny of the majority. In any case the result is that the children have been so to speak banished from the world of grown-ups. They are either thrown back upon themselves or handed over to the tyranny of their own group, against which, because of its numerical superiority, they cannot rebel, with which, because they are children, they cannot reason, and out of which they cannot flee to any other world because the world of adults is barred to them. The reaction of the children to this pressure tends to be either conformism or juvenile delinquency and is frequently a mixture of both.

This last sentence defines present-day conditions in Britain. She goes on to say: 'That modern education, in so far as it attempts to establish a world of children, destroys the necessary conditions for vital development and growth seems obvious.' Her definition of the necessary authority invested in teachers is perhaps the most famous part of her essay:

> In so far as the child is not yet acquainted with the world, he must be gradually introduced to it; in so far as he is new, care must be taken that this new thing comes to fruition in relation to the world as it is. In any case, however, the educators here stand in relation to the young as representatives of a world for which they must assume responsibility although they themselves did not make it, and even though they may, secretly or openly, wish it were other than it is. This responsibility is not arbitrarily imposed upon educators; it is implicit in the fact that the young are introduced by adults into a continuously changing world. Anyone who refuses to assume joint responsibility for the world should not have children and must not be allowed to take part in educating them.

> In education this responsibility for the world takes the form of authority. The authority of the educator and the qualifications of the teacher are not the same thing. Although a measure of qualification is indispensable for authority, the highest possible qualification can never by itself beget authority. The teacher's qualification consists in knowing the world and being able to instruct others about it, but his authority rests on his assumption of responsibility for that world. Vis-à-vis the child it is as though he were a representative of all adult inhabitants, pointing out the details and saying to the child: This is our world.

Today it is obvious that teachers and parents fear this authority. It is as though parents daily said: 'In this world even we are not very securely at home, how to move about in it, what to know, what skills to master, are mysteries to us too. You must try to make out as best you can, in any case you are not entitled to call us to account. We are innocent, we wash our hands of you.' The *Black Papers* have been repeatedly attacked for linking progressive education with the growth of juvenile delinquency. Hannah Arendt's support of our view is based on common sense. The need for adults to assume authority for educational and moral standards is urgent if we are to save our society from inevitable decline.

Children need security. They want to know what the rules are. Schools exist to teach children literacy and numeracy, a body of knowledge and skills with which they can earn a living, to develop independence of mind, the ability to think clearly, the imaginative faculties and an awareness of the great achievements of our culture. Children do not know what they ought to learn or how to develop their abilities, nor are they born with settled habits of concentration. If the child through the discovery method can find out what he wants to know then the truant running free is the wisest of us all.

Teachers who do not teach, maintain reasonable discipline, and provide a structured, time-tabled, classroom environment are not only exploiting those who pay rates and taxes. They are also exploiting the children, and causing them considerable unhappiness.

As Professor Lynn illustrates, children are naturally competitive. They enjoy and thrive on reasonable competition, and to refuse marks, examinations and class lists will deprive them of educational stimulus and satisfaction. Teachers who bring their non-competitive political ideas into the classroom harm the children they are supposed to help.

Schools should recognise their responsibility to fit a pupil into the community: he is not an island.

Respect for country, elders, and reasonable and elected authority are part of his structure. Religious education was also built into the 1944 Act as an aid and not a penance. Nature abhors a vacuum, and if a child is brought up in a so-called value-free and religion-free environment then he is not only deprived but is available to be taken over by some anti-social creed which could destroy him, his family and his community. It is urgent that teachers, social workers and all involved with young people should understand their responsibilities and the nature of the authority they represent.

We need the maximum amount of variety and freedom in education, and we are pleased to publish Max Beloff's honest account of problems and successes at Buckingham. The article by Caroline Cox, Keith Jacka, and John Marks defines precisely the difference between traditional academic and Marxist attitudes towards knowledge. The dangers inherent in the Marxist approach make it increasingly urgent that its opponents should publicise their opinions. The *Black Papers* have given heart to thousands of teachers who agree with our sense of priorities and with the 'academic' approach to knowledge. We urge them to continue the struggle by writing letters to newspapers, publishing articles and taking part in public debate.

THE EDITORS

When is discrimination?

H. J. EYSENCK

Discrimination on racial, religious, or sexual grounds is rightly abhorrent to most of us; no one who, like the author, has seen at first hand the effects such discrimination has on individuals and groups (as in Nazi Germany) can have any doubts that it is incompatible with civilised life, with ethical principles, or with simple decency. Discrimination is a foul, evil, intolerable assault on all our values, and the Law is rightly taking a closer interest than ever in its prevention. All this makes it imperative that we should be aware of the nature of discrimination, be able to detect it, and not be misled into seeking it out where it does not exist. This short article attempts to point out some common errors into which otherwise well-meaning persons have frequently fallen, errors which may have the untoward effect of actually harming the cause of those on whose behalf efforts are being made in this connection.

Let us begin by looking at two diametrically opposed views of discrimination. The first view considers discrimination to have occurred when one person is preferred to another not on objective and relevant grounds, such as training, intelligence, talent, etc., but on grounds of colour, sex, or religion. Such discrimination contradicts what I would regard as one of the primary principles underlying civilised life, namely the principle that choice among candidates should always and entirely be made on objective and relevant grounds. Such grounds might of course include colour, sex, or religion; one would not engage a male to play the nurse in *Romeo and Juliet*, or a white man to play Joe Louis in a film about the black boxer, or a Muslim to teach religion in a Church of England school. But such cases are rare, and even there, of course, boys played female parts in Shakespeare's time, Olivier played the Moor in *Othello*, and our religious teaching might be less insular if we were less restrictive in our choice of teachers. It would not be sufficient to state that the grounds of selection should be objective; cases have been reported where American labour unions have insisted on the use of irrelevant intelligence tests to keep out black workers (who on average score 15 points lower in such tests) in spite of the fact that high scores in an intelligence test were irrelevant to the job in hand. Relevance therefore is important, and in the USA the Law in fact insists on the demonstration of such relevance.

An entirely different, and in my view mistaken, view of discrimination considers the case for the occurrence of discrimination proven whenever there are, in any selection procedure, differences in the ratio of successful to unsuccessful candidates which are related to race (or sex, or religion, or social class, or whatever kind of discrimination we are concerned with). Thus it is a well-known fact that in this country black children are over-represented in ESN classes, compared with their

number in the whole population; this, it is often suggested, is evidence of discrimination. The question of objective and relevant characteristics which might justify such a preponderance of black children in these classes is not even raised. In a similar manner, there are many publications demonstrating that female professors are few and far between, and the conclusion is reached that this disproportion is evidence of discrimination. It is of course entirely possible that these cases of disproportion are in fact due to discrimination; what I am suggesting here is simply that the facts of disproportion, without any further evidence, cannot be used to argue about their causes. An example may clarify this argument.

Let us say that a basketball team is to be selected from the young men of two large African tribes, the alphas and the betas, in order to play an American guest team. All the players are selected from the alphas, and there are no betas on the team—not even in the reserves. Is this evidence of discrimination? Suppose that the alphas are all Watusis, a tribe with a mean height of 7 feet, while all the betas are pygmies, with a mean height of 4 feet. Is not the disproportion in selection justified by the demonstrated, objective and relevant difference in height? Nor need we worry about the question of whether this difference is genetic or environmental; it is in fact genetic, but even if it were environmental, our choice would still have to take into account the all-too-visible difference in height between the tribes.

It might be said that, in education at least, no sensible person would make such an elementary mistake. This is not so; both in the USA and here many educators have in fact protested about the disproportion between blacks and whites in ESN classes, in specially advanced classes, in University admissions, and in similar advanced or retarded groups, and have suggested that the fact of disproportion itself is evidence of discrimination. A clear and interesting example of this type of thinking occurs in a book by the eminent and highly respected French sociologist Raymond Boudon, entitled *Education, Opportunity, and Social Inequality*. He uses the term 'social inequality' in the sense of discrimination, and defines this as follows: 'By inequality of social opportunity (IEO) I mean the differences in level of educational attainment according to social background . . . Thus a society is characterised by a certain amount of IEO if, for instance, the probability of going to college is smaller for a worker's son than for a lawyer's son.' Boudon does not even raise the question of whether such differences as are observed may not be due to genetic differences in intelligence—although he does note that within the working-class groups, for instance, expectation of going to college is a function of IQ! In other words, Boudon suggests that the fact that all classes are not represented equally in our universities is due to discrimination, and that absence of such discrimination, and of inequality of social opportunity, can only be demonstrated by complete equality of achievement. That such a nonsensical pronouncement can be made by a very able Professor of Social Sciences, widely read and sufficiently influential to have his books translated into English (and greeted with rapturous applause) indicates that the effort to define discrimination properly may not be a task of supererogation.

It is very relevant to this discussion to note that all the official indices of discrimination are in fact of precisely this kind; we are told that discrimination exists because there are disproportions between blacks and whites, men and women, middle-class and working-class children, in ESN or advanced classes, in university or polytechnic, in this or that employment; we are never told whether these disproportions may not be due to objective and relevant causes, rather than prejudice and discrimination. Yet without this further information the observed facts are meaningless; discrimination may or may not be present, but the figures quoted cannot establish its presence or absence. The small number of female professors, for instance, may be due to the fact that the majority of women have children, and that this simple process is a severe handicap in the competitive struggle for excellence in research, teaching, and maintaining up-to-date knowledge in ever-expanding fields. If appointments are made on an objective basis of achievement, knowledge, and proven teaching skill acquired over the years, the disproportion might (or might not) be explained in those terms, rather than in terms of discrimination.

It might be argued that such presumptions of discrimination, without proper proof, do no harm, but this would be far from true. In the first place, they provoke resentment and thus produce divisiveness; to have one's child sent to an ESN class for objective reasons (because of scholastic backwardness, and in order to overcome such difficulties) is one thing; it is quite another to be told that this is done only because of racial discrimination. In the second place, such doctrines and assumptions promote official actions which are contrary to natural justice; they promote what they are designed to prevent, namely racial discrimination, and lead to even worse divisiveness. A good example of this is the doctrine of 'affirmative action' in the USA; it is now lawful for the government and its agencies to insist that 'minorities' should be represented proportionately among employees of firms receiving over a certain minimum of money from the Federal Government. ('Minorities' is put in quotes because many minorities, such as the Jews, are not so protected, and other 'minorities' which are included in the provisions of the law are in fact majorities, like women! Such illogicalities do not seem to worry the proponents of this far-reaching legislation.)

In effect this amounts to the institution of a quota system; it is of interest to educationists because practically all American universities and colleges are subject to this law. This has led to much unfair discrimination against white candidates for university positions, with the result that black candidates are often chosen in spite of much lower scholastic records, poorer research records, and less teaching experience. A recent experiment illustrates this rather well; it is reported in *Race* (Vol. 15, p. 106 *et seq*). A fictitious curriculum vitae for a graduate student of Washington University was concocted and used to apply for positions at 176 American universities; in half the applications the race of the applicant (black) was mentioned. The response rate for the putative black candidate was greater than for the candidate whose race was not mentioned (61 per cent v. 48 per cent); moreover, in their replies 44 per cent of the universities expressed active interest in pursuing the application of the black candidate, while less than 10 per cent expressed a similar interest for the other candidate! Thus affirmative action produces a very strong bias in favour of black applicants; such a person's chances to obtain a position, *with identical qualifications*, are six times as great as those of a person of undisclosed race! This is indeed racialism and discrimination with a vengeance, all by courtesy of a democratic government! (The impression given by this experiment is borne out in detail by reports of former students of mine who now hold established chairs in American universities; they all report precisely this sort of response to applications by black students, and the acceptance of even persons of low competence, in preference to whites of much competence.)

Similar considerations apply to student acceptance. In view of the average inferiority of black applicants on any scholastic admittance tests, many universities now operate different criteria for black and white students, with the result that competent white students are excluded in favour of less competent black students. The outcome of this racialist policy of discrimination is of course predictable: as long as identical standards are set for degree examinations, the great majority of the black students unfortunately have been found to fail, often at a low level. This sets up hostility between white and black students, and the hoped-for increase in fraternisation has in fact not taken place. In its stead we have experienced exactly the opposite. Blacks and whites now form separate blocks in most universities, implacably hostile to each other, with bitter talk of racial discrimination going in both directions. In some universities the outcome has been to treat whites and blacks differently as far as examination results are concerned, with blacks achieving pass grades with much lower grade points and marks than whites. Alternatively, special 'easy' subjects are introduced for blacks, to enable them to pass; 'black studies' is one such set of courses. All of this exacerbates existing divisiveness, and is clearly contrary to natural justice and the doctrine of non-discrimination.

It gives me no pleasure to detail these disastrous consequences of mistaken kindness; those who take the view here criticised are at one with their critics in attempting to do the best they can in trying to ameliorate the sad and indeed terrible state of blacks and other 'disadvantaged' groups in our society. Criticism is not of their motives, which are identical with ours; it is of their lack of concern for facts which must decide, however unwelcome they may be, what is the best course to be

pursued for all concerned. It is sad that the motives of those who feel unhappy about the confusion caused by kind-hearted but ignorant progressives are often impugned; the argument is about means, not about ends; and it should be conducted on a factual basis. We all want to help the disadvantaged; our disagreement is on the best way to do it. To pretend that all are equal when patently this is not so may garner for the protagonist many a bouquet in political circles, but it only makes matters worse for the dull, the poor, the ignorant. A child is not sent to an ESN class as punishment, or as a gesture of discrimination; the child is given a chance to catch up with his peers when patently he is falling behind in ordinary class-work. Society goes out of its way to make possible this special tuition; it is meant as a help towards greater achievement, not a device for keeping him back. A poor-quality student is not *punished* by failing to gain admission to a university; he is prevented from wasting years of his life, and suffering humiliating failure, provided that the selection procedure is fair and relevant. It is no kindness to him to change the rules for his sake, and make him suffer failure and disappointment. In these matters realism must be combined with compassion; realism without compassion is a betrayal of our ethical and moral duty; compassion without realism is a betrayal of our duty to protect the interest of those who cannot do so themselves.

In schools, the attempt to equate numbers of black and white children in ESN or advanced classes in accordance with the number of black and white families in the community has led to some very strange developments. Thus in some states the use of IQ tests has been legally forbidden, and in others there are legal requirements for properly proportionate numbers of whites and blacks in different schools and classes. The outcome has been bedlam, with blacks who ought to be in ESN classes taking part in ordinary class sessions, without being able to understand what was going on, or black children in ordinary classes who are advanced, without rhyme or reason, to high level classes, simply in order to keep the proportions straight. The result was of course truanting, vandalism, and violence, to an extent even experienced teachers had never before encountered. Finally, in many cases (e.g. Black House and Casa de la Raza) coloured parents, infuriated by these results of 'liberal' policies, demanded (and got) segregated schools for coloureds only—thus does failure to define discrimination properly lead to failure in the important programme of desegregation, and its effective reversal by precisely those whom it was designed to benefit!

The question of 'busing', i.e. driving (usually black) children out of their neighbourhood into better white neighbourhoods in order to integrate with the school system there, to reduce 'discrimination', is also relevant here. The results have on the whole been disappointing; there has been if anything a sharpening of racial tension and conflict, no lessening of differences in achievement, and often a lowering of performance in both groups. Berkeley was among the first to achieve complete integration, and its busing scheme was held up to the nation as exemplary; what have been the consequences? Michael Grant, who has made a close study of the situation in Berkeley, has described the result graphically in the *National Review* (16 May 1973).

The original idea, perhaps possible only here in the capital of theoretical liberalism, was that black ghetto students, rubbing elbows with bright, highly motivated white students, would see the beauty of white middle-class standards and begin to perform better. Exactly the reverse happened. Those nice white middle-class highly motivated students embraced the standards of the ghetto, and in the high schools and junior high schools, the hoodlum types became the leaders.

Shakedowns, fights, robberies, bomb threats, and beatings have become the order of the day in Berkeley's high schools. Dope is peddled openly and routinely on school grounds, and sexual abuses during school hours are as common as sock hops used to be in the Fifties. Each month brings a new wave of rapes, faithfully recorded by the Berkeley Daily Gazette. A blind girl is raped in the halls of Berkeley High. Another girl, raped on the floor, screams to students passing by for help. They ignore her. Needless to say, in such an atmosphere very little learning goes on. David DuPree, a black feature writer for the *Wall Street Journal*, describes what he saw at Berkeley High when he enrolled as a student. In one classroom students sat around playing records, drinking wine, and smoking marijuana. Students wandered in and out of other classes, which they are free to attend or not, as they choose. (They graduate anyhow). 'They look at all this freedom as meaning you can get something for nothing,' one disillusioned educator told DuPree. 'They think they're shaking the white man up just hanging around and still graduating.'

These are some of the results of the all-too-frequent misunderstanding of the meaning of discrimination. Other types of 'counter-discrimination', i.e. favouring the under-privileged, are often suggested, such as, to have these children taught by the best teachers, under specially favourable conditions, e.g. with small pupil/teacher ratios. This was tried at the Raphael Well school in San Francisco (as well as in many other schools all over the USA). Project 'Learn Well' was designed for these mostly black children, and miraculous improvement in reading was promised. Standardised tests of achievement, however, showed that the results of the programme were quite the opposite. Most of the children had fallen behind in total reading skills rather than improved, and the appraisal of the programme called it 'a complete and utter failure'—in spite of the expenditure of large funds specially collected for this and similar ventures. Claims were made that behaviour had 'improved', but on-the-spot investigators testified that conditions resembled bedlam as compared with suburban schools, where the expenditures per pupil were actually less, and the class sizes nearly double, but achievement was good.

Inverted racial discrimination has been responsible, not only for such antidemocratic practices as 'affirmative action', busing, and the like, but also for what a recent Stanford University report calls 'racism without racists' (this is the actual title of the report by Professor Sanford Dornbusch). 'In the past, many teachers expressed overt hostility towards minority students in their classrooms,' the report states. 'Teachers now are expressing warmth towards minority students, without accompanying their friendliness with challenging academic standards. This is just as debilitating to students as the old overt hostility . . .' There was, for these children, an almost complete divorce between effort and achievement, on the one hand, and grades, praise and encouragement on the other. Children did not believe that they would get poor grades if they did poor work, or did not try. 'Grades were seen more as a carrot than a stick'—in other words, when just being there ensures good grades, there is no threat of poor work resulting in poor grades.

All this may seem a long way from conditions in this country, but trends started in the USA have a habit of catching up with us. Already there are many similar proposals floating about; already mistaken views about alleged discrimination in assigning coloured children to ESN classes are widely publicised. Measures similar to the American ones mentioned above are suggested in relation to differences in social class, examinations, and other issues. If we do not look out, the consequences of an erroneous definition of discrimination will catch up with us, making life, achieve-ment and success desperately more difficult to reach, not only for one group of children, but for all.

Is it really true that we learn nothing from history, except that we learn nothing from history? What has happened in America should always be before our eyes, teaching us that however admirable might be the motives of kind-hearted reformers, the effects of their actions may be, and often are, catastrophic, destroying existing practices that have always worked well, and failing to put in their stead anything that works even half as well. Nor do these changes benefit those whom they are supposed to benefit; the underprivileged, the poor, the coloured often suffer even more than other members of the community. The answer to the question: 'When is discrimination?' is not an easy one, but it is desperately important that we should not get it wrong.

The threat to religion

E. R. NORMAN

When, in May 1976, the Religious Education Council recommended radical changes in the nature of religious education in the nation's schools, the public first became aware of ideas which had for ten years been acquiring ready acceptance amongst theorists of education and leading churchmen. For some time before that, of course, groups of Humanist intellectuals had been contending that Christian instruction should be stripped out of the curriculum. In the 1960s, no doubt to their astonishment and delight, they found both their ideas, and the very rhetoric in which they expressed them, suddenly reproduced in the apologetics of Church leaders. Sir Richard Acland's book, *We Teach Them Wrong*, pub-lished in 1963, was a harbinger of things to come. There he assailed Christian teaching for being a 'propaganda experience', unsuited to the modern intelligence. He suggested a revolution in the whole approach to religious education. At the time his tract passed off easily enough as a period piece—it was the period of the Bishop of Woolwich's evidence in the *Lady Chatterley* trial and of *Honest to God*. But the spores multiplied and began to germinate all over the place.

In 1970 the Commission set up jointly by the Church of England's Board of Education and the National Society (the body to which nearly all Church schools are affiliated) reported sympathetically to the new ideas. Its chairman was Dr

Ian Ramsey, Bishop of Durham, a committed political and theological radical. The Durham Report envisaged religious *education* (rather than *instruction*) which neither 'indoctrinated' the children nor 'imposed' any religious beliefs upon them. Religious education was to become an 'act of exploration . . . it must endeavour to provide for the possibility of built-in self-criticism so as to anticipate from the start the possibility of reasoned choice.' Moral education, too, was to be on an 'open' basis, to avoid moral 'authoritarianism' and the 'conditioning' of children. From this point, the concept of 'open' religious education entered the canon of orthodoxy. Its almost immediate academic prestige has been such that virtually no other scheme for religious education is now put forward in teacher training colleges. Almost the whole of the educational establishment appears to regard the 'new RE' as self-evidently right. Humanist intellectuals have had their work unexpectedly done for them by excited enthusiasts within the world of religious education itself.

Thus the provision of religious instruction in the 1944 Education Act looks like turning into something of a Trojan horse. Without any change in the law, the new ideas began to filter into the system. Public disquiet came first over the row in Birmingham caused by proposals for a new agreed syllabus in religious education, published in 1973. The Birmingham scheme enshrined many of the progressive ideals. Christianity was to lose its special place in religious education, and other religions, together with 'non-religious stances for living', were to be presented to the children with equal weight. The press became agitated because Communism was to be one of the 'non-religious stances'. But there can be little doubt that in this, and similar enterprises now in preparation, it is Humanism which will be the greatest beneficiary. It will replace Christianity as the 'established' creed in the schools—with the symbols of establishment as well. For the daily act of worship, also required by the 1944 Act, has come under fire as an illiberal preference for Christianity. In many schools, already, the day no longer opens with the familiar hymns and Bible readings, but with extracts from approved moralists of the century: from Gandhi, Dag Hammarskjöld, Martin Luther King, Mao Tse Tung, etc. (J. F. Kennedy, once in this list, is now usually omitted because of press revelations about the exact nature of his moral discernment.) In 1975 a book which has been extensively praised by educational theorists was published by the Student Christian Movement Press: *School Worship. An Obituary*. Its author is an Australian, Dr John Hull, Lecturer in Religious Education at Birmingham University. He maintains that in school assemblies there should be 'no more intimate connection between religious education and the assembly than there would be between any other subject and the assembly'. It is, indeed, the right occasion for showing 'slides of urban problems', and for presenting the 'humanitarian aspects' of world issues. There are to be readings 'from the writings of Confucius, Mao Tse Tung, and the Chinese poets and philosophers'. This is because 'few schools can now claim to be Christian communities'.

It is, in fact, the assertion that England is now a 'pluralistic' society which lies at the basis of the case for secularising the schools. The case is made, therefore, upon grounds of civil liberty—that it is wrong in principle to 'indoctrinate' children into religious attitudes when society itself regards religious belief as controversial. In several variations, this is the case which recurs many times in a 1975 publication called *New Movements in Religious Education*, a series of essays on the 'new RE', edited by Professor Ninian Smart, Head of the Religious Studies Department at Lancaster University. In his preface to the collection, Professor Smart wrote that 'the 1944 Education Act clearly was not succeeding, and the ever-increasing pluralism of British society demanded a fresh approach.' Britain was now a 'multi-belief society'. With barely-concealed pleasure, many of the theorists of the new approach fall upon the existence of immigrant communities as practical evidence of their contentions. How can it be right to conduct a school as a Christian institution when a large part of the intake may consist of Hindus, Sikhs or Moslems? It is argued that it is the duty of the parents, or the Churches, to inculcate Christianity; the job of the school is to prepare children only for a knowledge of their cultural inheritance—to teach *about* religion and other 'life stances'. Some of the enthusiasts for change point to the deficient quality of some existing religious instruction. This is sometimes represented as a reluctance by teachers to become involved in the 'hypocrisy' of teaching *as true* things which are not widely believed in society. In their foreword (which they call a 'Backword') to *A Bedside Book for RE Teachers* (SCM, 1975), Terence Copley and Donald Easton write: 'tub-thumping Christianisers can leave the classroom and buy a Do-It-Yourself home pulpit kit'. And of the new religious education they declare: 'This is the subject for the teacher interested in religious insights (from all religions), in non-religious stances for living such as humanism, even in anti-religious stances such as some brands of communism.' Both in tone and in substance, this is a good summary of the new orthodoxies.

What does it all amount to? It should, in the first place, be noticed that the primary justification for the shift in attitudes to religious teaching is, to say the least, open to question. For England is *not* a 'pluralistic' society, except in a most qualified sense. It is, on the contrary, a society whose leaders of opinion have lost confidence in their own traditional values and who represent the resulting chaos as a reasoned diversity. Nearly all the 'life stances' of the 'pluralistic' society turn out to be located within a small section. Humanism, Marxism, and so on, are characteristics of the intelligentsia, and of those who have been induced to suppose it a sign of maturity to simulate them. Unhappily the teaching profession—and those who train teachers—are especially open to the 'crisis of values'. It is they who most easily become compulsive moralists for their own new moral diversities; who seek to pass on their own sense of a 'crisis of values' to the children they teach. Critics of traditional religious instruction are always declaring that their pupils just don't want to be taught religion—that they are sceptical of religion, too much at home in the modern world. But children don't naturally reject inherited values: they are being *taught* to think like that, by teachers who have themselves adopted the fashionable scepticism of the bourgeois culture to which they belong. Fortunately the values of the home are very durable. Many children must come to regard the contemporary moral agonising of the classroom—all the indoctrination into the liberal idealism of moral diversity—as a peculiarity of the school world, not really in correspondence with reality. Their teachers also propagate some pretty dogmatic liberalism, too, and this must seem oddly at variance with their paraded belief in the legitimacy of diverse 'stances for living'. The notion of a 'pluralism' of values is the present form in which the social class differences between the teachers and the taught now appear. For working-class and lower-middle-class society show few signs of religious or moral diversity. There are far more Humanists and Communists within the middle classes than there are in the working classes. The diversities of life styles turn out, of course, to be class characteristics of the bourgeoisie. Teaching children to regard morality as a matter of reasoned choice is, therefore, a species of embourgeoisement.

It is true that a large majority of parents are not themselves church-goers. It is equally true, however, that they expect their children to be taught Christianity in the schools—opinion polls have been decisive in showing that. In this connection it is helpful to realise that the immigrant communities are too small a minority to disturb the overall picture. The West Indians are anyway Christians: often more faithful ones than the native population. The much-publicised problem about teaching religion to the immigrant children only arises in those areas, themselves not very great in number, where Asian settlement is concentrated. It is no argument for 'pluralism' to latch on to the existence of a tiny minority of the school population. Many parents, in their aspirations for their children's education into 'solid' values, equate Christianity with 'decency'. It is the form which their moral sense takes. That, too, has been much derided by theorists of religious education. It is as well to observe, therefore, that it is not just the 'nominal' Christianity of the parents which does this: the whole emphasis of contemporary academic theology has been leaning towards the identification of 'God' with the prevalent notions of secular moral seriousness. That was what the 1960s conflation of Humanism and Christianity—so much approved by Church leaders at the time—was all about. Yet Christianity, traditionally understood Christianity, remains the basic reference for the serious moments in most people's lives. That is why so very many parents, though they do not support the Churches, at least by attending them, seek to have their children taught the truth of Christian values. Since the educational system of this country is the authoritative place in which the nation's values are passed on, it is obvious to expect that parents will wish Christianity, and not some balancing act of moral diversities, to be the concrete form which the teaching of values takes.

The argument about the alleged minority status of Christianity in modern society is an odd one to find deployed by educationalists for another reason. Are they really maintaining that ideals and value-systems which do not enjoy a predominance must all be presented to the children as enjoying a parity of worth, leaving the children to make their own choice? Are racism or anti-Semitism to be presented alongside other values as if equal? Dr John Hull is unprepared for anything so serious as *politics* to be left to the free choice of children (only religion is fit for that). School assemblies, he argues, should be used for 'the teaching of democracy'. They are to 'demonstrate the values which are not controversial and upon which democratic society depends'. It would be difficult to find which of the elements of 'democracy' are not regarded as controversial by some group or other in this 'pluralist' society. Somewhere a decision has to be made about precisely what values *are* to be given the authority of the classroom. That is the central difficulty, and it is an unresolved one. No one in 1944, at the time of the Education Act, could conceive that, in so few years, the leading theorists of religion would be interpreting 'religious instruction' as a licence to teach any moral values which happened to take the fancy of the high-minded. So no one felt it necessary to create a uniform system of deciding what the content of religious education should be. But the present assault upon the teaching of Christianity raises the problem in a particularly acute fashion. There is no doubt, however, about the overwhelming desire for Christian instruction, in a suitably non-sectarian form, felt by most parents.

The advocates of the 'new RE' have their own solution to the problem of determining which moral and religious ideas are to be taught in the schools. It is to teach several of them, on an 'open' basis, with no preference given to one over another—the children to 'think for themselves'. That is the centre-piece of the proposals for change. 'We live in a plural society where folk, even very young folk, have to make up their own

minds', according to Professor Smart. Or, in the words of Mr Peter Gedge, Head of Religious Studies at St Martin's College of Education, Lancaster, the teacher 'must respect the individual pupil's integrity and leave him really free to come to his own decisions'. But, for all the weight of authoritative opinion ranged in support of this proposition, it is difficult to see how in practice it can be applied. If children are really left to 'think for themselves' there will be a moral anarchy. Those most in need of education are simply not capable of educated choice. Nor do children bring to the task of moral and religious learning a mind capable of the sort of sophisticated manipulation of ideas which evidently delights the professional moralists of our day. In reality, of course, the moral and religious options presented to the children 'for choice' are carefully pre-selected. A specious 'choice' is then allowed *either* between several approved viewpoints, narrowly clustered together on the available spectrum of opinion, *or* between an approved position favourably represented and one so caricatured as to appear patently corrupt. It is a bogus private enterprise that the children are to be offered.

The whole notion of 'open' religious education, in fact, is just the device by which approved attitudes are indoctrinated; by which the teachers get their propaganda accepted by the children. In practice it will inevitably lead to the propagation of Humanist morality. It is that which is so frequently regarded as a sort of agreed morality by advocates of the 'new RE'. Genuine variations are *not* offered to the children 'for choice'. Thus in the Birmingham syllabus, Communism is to be taught but not Fascism. Yet Fascism has unquestionably been one of the most influential 'stances for living' of the twentieth century. Humanism, furthermore, is not an agreed morality. Both it, and the device by which it is to be disseminated in the schools, suggest a relativism in human moral judgment which is totally at variance with Christianity—whatever the trendy theologians may say. Humanist assertions about the part played by rationality in moral choice are opposed to the Christian view of human nature. One of the great evils of the 'open' approach to religious education is that it will actively result in the positive destruction of a lot of the children's religious faith, by throwing the authority of the school behind relativistic attitudes to the basic criteria by which moral and religious values are determined. Some influential theorists apparently suppose that young children are anyway incapable of the 'abstract' ideas involved in religious belief. It is a further indication of their ignorance of religion. For even if it were true, it would not touch Christianity because it is not 'abstract'. It is Incarnational. It is about a Person. It is about the real world of our sensations, taught by Christ Himself in earthly stories. It is only the radical theologians of the present time who have represented it as a quasi-Humanist contrivance of moralistic probabilities dependent upon intellectual assent to tentatively formulated abstract propositions. Is that the ephemeral version of Christianity which is to be taken as the religious position around which the discussion of Christian education is to turn? A quick glance at some of the material for RE classes published by the Student Christian Movement in recent years would suggest that it is. There the reader beholds the most monstrous caricatures of 'traditional' religion—appearing as class oppression, as insensitive to human material needs, as the dogmatic enemy of intellectual enlightenment. The Church's own apparently obsessive guilt, and loss of faith in its own unchanging values, do not help.

The 'open' approach to religious education, therefore, is not in reality very open in what it allows children to select. It could not be otherwise. Children do not think for themselves—except at the higher end of secondary education, where that sort of exercise might be quite valid. The proposed new syllabuses, furthermore, are likely to be much more prescriptive than the old ones. Compulsion is the method by which liberal enlightenment always secures the propagation of itself. What the children will eventually 'choose' will depend on the inclinations of the teacher who slants the information presented. It will inevitably produce great diversities—indeed it will help to create the 'pluralist' society whose existence is alleged in justification. I had reason last year, when I spoke on these matters at a public meeting, to see exactly how closed the 'new RE' may well become. During the question time which followed, a headmistress expressed her shocked disapproval of my support for 'traditional' Christian teaching. In her school, she contended, *all* viewpoints were presen-

ted with balance and equal fairness. But, she added, her opposition to my opinions was such that she 'could not even begin to discuss them' with me. It was a rare moment of truth.

It is worth pointing out, incidentally, that *moral education* raises precisely the same problem as *religious* education. For some time now it has been developing as an autonomous subject—a tendency assisted by the work and research of the Schools Council Moral Education Project, set up in 1972. But exactly the same sort of objections now adduced in respect to the teaching of Christianity in the schools must logically apply against morality taught in a secular frame of reference: that in a 'pluralistic' society no preference can be given to one position over another. The fact that the position at issue may be *secular* does not make it *neutral*. And anyway, an attempt at an agreed secular moral scheme will be to 'establish' either some new brand of Natural Law doctrine, or a version of Humanism.

Another point seems appropriate. Occasionally complaints are made by parents that the ideals and attitudes given under the guise of religious education, in schools which have already gone over to the 'new RE' (as very many have), are politically partisan. They complain of left-wing bias. These sorts of reservation are pretty summarily discounted. A complaint made against a London comprehensive school in 1972 was dismissed by the governors, but got some adverse press publicity. Yet there is no doubt that the rhetoric and images used to propagate moral idealism in the schools sometimes *are* the same as those of the political Left. It is another illustration of the assumption that progressive and Humanist ideas are self-evidently true. When questioned about this sort of thing, teachers rationalise their emotional commitments; they reason away the style of their propaganda as merely a convenient manner of expressing moral truths about human society shared by all men of good will. It further indicates the fraudulent nature of the freedom of 'choice' open to the children.

It is clear that, whatever the diversities of outlook said to exist within the intelligentsia, it is Christianity which remains the nearest thing there is in this country to an agreed morality. For the vast majority of parents, Christian truth is the basis of the personal moral order they would most like to see their children learn at school. The future should not, therefore, lie with the opinionated minority who clamour for a secularisation of the nation's educational system. It should be given to an improvement of the present provision of religious instruction. There is an astonishing ignorance in our society of what Christian doctrines actually *are*. The Churches are doubtless much to blame for this, especially today, when they are more absorbed by social issues than they are by eternal ones. The 1944 Education Act made wise provision for religious instruction. It should be fulfilled, not abandoned. The Act has come to be understood by advocates of change as an attempt by a Christian society of the past to safeguard beliefs which are no longer widely subscribed. That is a misunderstanding. It was not how those who enacted the legislation saw it at all—as reference to *Hansard* will verify. The religious provisions were intended as an initiative to Christianise society, to make people *more* aware of Christianity, not merely to hold the line. There is no evidence to suggest that, however much the intelligentsia may have traded in their values for new ones since then, the mass of the people do not still see that as its purpose. The conscience clause still protects those who do not want Christian instruction. In very many schools religious instruction is being given both sensitively and intelligently, relating the content and manner of teaching to peculiarities of environment and circumstance. In those places where concentrated Asian settlement has produced a genuinely multi-faith society there will naturally have to be special provision for the teaching of their own religious values in the schools. But there is no need to abandon the whole structure within which such practical *ad hoc* exceptions are required. As in the past, so in the future there will doubtless be resistance from children—as there is to learning other subjects in the curriculum, and as there is to being taught Humanist morality. Indeed, children have a built-in distrust of moralisers of whatever pedigree, as the practitioners of the 'new RE' will discover. There are no inexorable pressures making it impossible to continue teaching Christianity in the schools—only a powerful lobby from a small section of society addicted to highly unstable fashions of thinking.

Some advice to the Churches: hold on to the Voluntary Aided Schools and ignore the Durham Report. If the state system *should* become secularised it would be a great pity, to say the least, if only those parents able to pay for private education could send their children to a school with Christian instruction. The Church schools were founded and endowed—originally largely by private donation—with the explicit obligation to associate the acquisition of secular learning with religious truth. It would not be honest to depart from that intention while there are still many who support it.

The question of religion in the schools is one of immense seriousness. What sort of society is it which allows educational theorists to put its inherited values up for auction in the classroom? The values of this country are under threat. Society discloses advanced symptoms of moral collapse, as the opinions of the intelligentsia seep downwards. Nations of high morale and with confidence in their values never allow children to 'choose' their 'stance for living'. Our own evident preparedness to countenance such an idea (however much the practice may be frustrated by a hidden guidance into approved attitudes) is a sure indication of our sickness. It describes a society which could easily succumb to any set of values presented in the manner appropriate to its expectations. This is a society in the act of destroying its own moral authority by purporting to resign from prescriptive moral norms in the classroom. The protagonists of the new methods and ideals see themselves in the vanguard of a higher moral maturity: where rationality reigns, even children may freely choose their own beliefs. But it is a moral relativism they are in danger of fostering. Fashions in moral idealism now come and go with great rapidity, each one acclaimed in its brief moment of acceptance as the distillation of wisdom. As each in turn is palmed off on the children by their teachers a great moral chaos will accumulate within a few decades—if the whole absurdity is allowed to go on that long. In the wings the hard men of ideology are waiting to come on. Why should they interfere now, while their work of scorching the earth in preparation for the new crop is being done so effectively for them? Doubtless it would be preferable to dispense with religious education altogether, rather than see it transformed in the present manner.

That, however, will not happen. The religious education industry, in the universities and colleges of education, has far too great a vested interest to allow that. Their compulsive moralising yearns for expression. In the end, perhaps, it will be possible still to count on the values of the home winning against the influence of the teachers of morals. But it is something of a race against time.

Artful dodgers of the world—unite

RON LEWIS

After Flower Power, Pupil Power, Gay Power, what was more natural than Villain Power?

Mind you, when my house was broken into recently, I found some difficulty in consoling myself with the thought that the person responsible was in the vanguard of the class struggle. Yet I am enjoined to believe this by no less authoritative a body than the National Association of Probation Officers' Action Group, a small but influential group of Probation Officers having affinity with the International Socialists, who, by pressure group tactics, have managed to dominate the National Association of Probation Officers' Conferences and seriously change the direction of the Association. Their view is also shared by the sort of academic who gives support to the group National Deviancy Conference, a prominent member of which, Roy Bailey, I heard addressing a day conference of social workers with these words—'theft is a bourgeois concept'. (At question-time I wished him an early break-in!)

Not that talking rubbish about crime hasn't been with us for some time. When I was training to be a probation officer (which is so long ago as to be almost pre-Marcuse), housebreaking was described by a tutor in psychiatry as symbolically a furtive exploration of a woman's body—if committed by an early post-pubertal boy; breaking into gas meters—an act of penetration; taking and driving away—an orgasmic experience. But at least the madness concept of delinquency, as the Freudian 'era' came to be called (to distinguish it from its predecessor—the badness concept) had the merit of not making a virtue out of naughtiness.

Some confusion about crime is understandable. Today's middle aged were weaned on the concept that crime was an outcome of poverty and ignorance. Since Beveridge took care of the first, and Butler the second, disappointment was inevitable, with a crime-rate in the affluent society several times that of hard-faced pre-war capitalist Britain. One might have hoped that by now, somebody might be going back to the drawing-board if only to tremble on the brink of considering whether the very reforms intended to abolish crime are actually generating it. No such luck, however. All that the political parties seem to have as a response to the growing problem of crime is terminological abolition. Already, the under 17s have been decriminalised (their offences of mugging and housebreaking accounting for about 25 per cent of all such offences are merely cries for help).

Most of the new entrants into social work are coming via university or polytechnic courses, unlike the old days when they were frequently 'retreads' from other walks of life; already, the selection decision concerning suitability for social work is being made more by the academic institutions than by the services concerned; already we see social workers and probation officers behaving as though they were self-employed, seeking to develop their own goals. Such is the homage paid to education and professionalism in contemporary society, that those with formal control over the activities of social workers, such as Social Service and Probation and After-Care Committees, seem reluctant to exercise it in matters other than pro-visioning. Such too, is the legitimate concern to preserve academic freedom that little if anything is done to influence the content of social work train-ing. The result is that we are in serious danger as a community of seeing our institutions and values changed, not by the will of the people, but by the actions of the paid servants of the community.

Related to the problem is the general situation of social work. This is characterised by a rate of growth arising out of the Seebohm revolution which has been such that the traditions of the various groups of social workers existing before this development (largely working in small groups, if not alone) have been swept aside by the flood of new entrants. Even in the Probation Service, the best organised, trained and ideologically equipped of the old services, only about a third have more than three years' service. I do not suggest neces-sarily that more means worse, but it certainly means different. And services expanding at such a rate inevitably tend to become a continuation of the university experience by other means, i.e. one newly qualified graduate rapidly adapts to the needs and traditions of the agency; half a dozen transform it into an adjunct of the campus.

Given the contemporary social attitude of seek-ing wisdom at the shrine of the cradle, it is scarcely surprising that those with responsibility to manage social work are currently having such a tough time. For a start, they do not really know how to assess the behaviour of their new staff. There is a tendency to overlook faults—indeed to regard them as features of 'bright young graduates'. But even if they wished to react, such has been the competition for staff they couldn't afford to get the reputation of being 'square', authoritarian, or punitive. Furthermore, many of today's managers, certainly in the Probation Service, fought for years to get the professional status which the Central Council for the Education and Training of Social Workers provides, and are thus emotionally incapable of receiving bad news about it. Hence, every experiment, no matter how mani-festly inane, gets support; every idea, no matter

how foolish, is treated with awe and deemed to have significant content especially if it is incom-prehensible. The most salient feature of the social-work scene of today is the almost total abdication of reason!

If there is a reluctance (which I share) to inter-fere with academic freedom, no such reluctance inhibits some academics from interfering with us. A couple of years ago, a group of tutor Probation Officers in Kent, my own county, were told by the local university professor of social administration, that the old guard in the Service were either going to have to change, or get out. Repeated pleas come from academic tutors for the power to ensure that what they teach in the institutions is not disregar-ded by the services in which their erstwhile students obtain employment. In this attitude they themselves betray the spirit of academic freedom. For the claim of the traditional academic was that he trained minds to think; he made available the finer products of the human mind; but he did not seek ultimately to determine what his student thought, much less to direct his post-graduate life.

By far the most sinister manifestation of aca-demic interference with social work comes from the body calling itself the National Deviancy Con-ference. It describes itself as a quasi-academic body and was founded in 1968. Its founders were persons holding positions in social science and similar departments in various centres of higher education, and its purposes are to forge links with people active in radical social work. It operates by holding symposia, the chief message of which seems to be that good is bad—e.g. the act becomes deviant only when it is thus labelled by policemen, magistrates and journalists; and that bad is good—e.g. Manson, the Weathermen and vandals are simply demonstrating in action that an alterna-tive society based upon deviant values is possible. They also liaise with many of the fringe revolu-tionary groups, which having recruited few law-abiding people, now pursue the law-breakers. Such groups organise rent strikes, squatting, and give support to, if not actually organise, prison riots.

In a way, it almost does them an injustice to call them sinister. They are quite overt; their books are published by Penguin; one of their founders, Laurie Taylor, now regularly appears on the Robert Robinson chat show; and they are not short of platforms provided at the taxpayer's expense in the form of courses and day conferences. But the implications of this group are quite sinister. They are advocating, or giving support to, lawlessness, including acts of violence. And when one considers that those most affected by their activities are people like probation officers, whose function is to uphold the law, it is necessary to cry out—enough! For what they advocate is tantamount to an invitation to the policeman to burgle your home; the defence lawyer to plead for your conviction; or the doctor to take your life. No defence of academic freedom can justify so obscene a misuse of public funds.

The Probation Officers' Action Group referred to earlier, is a striking example of the success which these radical academics have achieved. This group, in the space of a few years, has placed itself in a commanding position within the professional association. The association is now committed to seeking closed-shop status; to the abolition of differentials between the managers and the basic grade officer; to refusal to work with 'political' offenders; to a statement that amounts to an attack upon the integrity of the judiciary, and to many other policies far too numerous to mention here that are wholly at variance with the traditions of the Service. They have succeeded by good organisation, the infectious appearance of enthusiasm, and the virtual absence of any official discouragement. The opposition to them within the association is disorganised and becomes manifest only during a referendum, the election of national officers (which is by postal ballot), and by voting with one's feet; only 65 per cent of officers are now in the association. The group also succeeded because the concept of academic freedom has been carried over into the work situation, although in this setting it survives under the name: professionalism. (One now realises how true was Shaw's definition of that word—a conspiracy against the laity.) In short, such is the state of scholarship today in the field of criminology that, with their cohesive philosophy, they appear to have all the good tunes.

To oppose them in public now is to court disaster. At the 1976 annual conference, I was myself denounced as a diabolical reactionary in public, and a fascist in private. Moderate friends of mine were cool towards me in public in case they should attract similar attacks. For, since the leadership of the Service remains silent, it is anybody's guess what the 'safe' attitude will turn out to be. The leadership of the Service is no doubt silent itself because of political uncertainties, which are not likely to be resolved while the economy remains in its present state; even though, it is not too fanciful to suggest, our present difficulties are not unrelated to the sloppiness, of which the matters I have raised are such a prime example.

I am certain that the present state of affairs in the Probation Service is related to current practices in education. Many of the lecturers, let alone their students, are themselves products of the Spockian era. Scant attention is paid in many social science departments to the transmission of the values and the ethos of our society—indeed, value-judgement is a four-letter word (is the opposite, *valueless* judgement?). Even where forces are at work less sinister than those I have been writing about, preoccupation with *change* tends to soften up the individual's resistance to bad ideas, for fear he will display a lack of flexibility. The declared aim of the staff development unit (part of the Probation Service) in my area, is to challenge traditional methods of work. The unit was responsible for a course I attended at Madingley Hall, Cambridge, in 1972, in which the whole week was given over to lecturers seeking to prove that all our work was a waste of time, and that the best that could be said for it was that it might be good for society's humanitarian image. In 1976, a three-day residential conference was given over to discussing the resistance to change of the management team of the Kent Probation Service. It was literally held that that resistance constituted the contemporary original sin. One could give many further examples of a continual chipping away at almost all belief, financed, it needs to be stressed, by the taxpayer. But to do so would reveal only how little has been achieved by a century of universal education and nearly a quarter of a century of mass higher education. For, far from increasing general resistance to priests, purveyors of the holy grail and other conmen, it has been reduced. The academic and the professional have not abolished the priest, they have simply stolen his clothes.

Crime may well be viewed for certain purposes as the outcome of complex and interacting factors. But for the practical purposes of those paid to manage the problem, it is essential that they perceive it to be an evil to be striven against, even though theirs will be a war without a total victory. Recognition that there may be bad or obsolete laws is not incompatible with an acknowledgement that the rule of law is a vital component of a civilised society: and given the freedom of our institutions to change the law, it is no excuse for giving aid to those who would change it by force.

It is in the giving of the authority of scholarship to fundamentally anti-social behaviour on the part of the semi-professions, that some of our higher educational establishments, in my view, betray the trust upon which their freedom to practise rests. I am certain, however, that while there are undoubtedly sinister forces at work in this situation, there are also bodies doing this by default, by,

dare one say it, poor scholarship! I would like to see those responsible for education itself take a hard look at what is being disseminated in colleges, polytechnics and universities in the name of social science, in the preparation of students for the semi-profession of social work, where, admittedly, the body of knowledge is scant. They might well consider that students' time might be better spent reading classical philosophy and great literature, not to mention history. At least then the student might leave college with respect for his heritage and an awareness of how long most of the short cuts in history turned out to be. He might also learn that much of what is described as new ways of thinking is really very old, and thus be better defended against the prophets of contemporary Marxism.

Competition and cooperation

RICHARD LYNN

The desirability of getting rid of competition and replacing it by cooperation is one of the most fundamental beliefs of progressive ideology. It is an idea that has made considerable headway in British education in recent decades, and is partly responsible for many of the changes that have taken place in British schools.

The central place of competition in the progressive demonology is too well known to need much documentation. 'We can begin at once in all schools to replace the ethic of competition and acquisition by one of cooperation and community' states a comprehensive school headmaster.[1] 'Elitist academic education fails because it fosters the values of competition rather than the values of cooperation' writes an educational psychologist.[2] 'The skills of cooperation are far more

crucial in today's world than are the skills of competition,' or so we are assured by a professor of education.[3] A chief education officer has recommended that school prizes should be abolished because they encourage unhealthy competitiveness.

This idea that competition is wrong is not simply a theory but has in recent years been put into practice in numerous schools throughout the country. It is probably the most important belief that lies behind the reduction in the emphasis placed on marks, prizes, streaming and examinations. All of these are seen as pressures stimulating the individual child to compete against his fellows. For this reason, according to progressive belief, they are wrong and should be reduced or abolished.

The problem of competition is a complex one,

and we shall have to consider whether individual competitiveness really is an important motivation for work, what are the side effects on those who fail, the relationship of competition and cooperation, and whether society would indeed be better if competitiveness were totally eliminated.

Individual competition as a motive to work

There is little doubt that individual competitiveness is a powerful motive to work, effort and achievement and that children will work harder when the situation is one of individual competition than when this motive is not called into play. Historically the first psychologist to demonstrate this seems to have been Moede in Germany just after the First World War.[4] He gave children the task of pulling on the handle of a dynamometer, a machine for measuring the strength of pull. First he took the children by themselves and had them endeavour to pull as hard as they could. Then he instructed the children to compete against each other to determine who could pull the hardest. The results showed that children exerted more effort in the second condition when they competed against each other.

Another of the early studies on competition was carried out in the early nineteen thirties by Pearl Greenberg in Vienna.[5] She worked with pairs of children between the ages of two and seven. She took both the children into a room and showed them a table with some bricks on it, and she asked them to build something with the bricks. The children began to build and when they had finished their efforts were assessed for general sophistication, e.g. size, structural ingenuity, etc. Then she pushed all the bricks into the middle of the table and said 'Now this time I would like to see who can build prettier'. This introduction of the competitive element seemed to have no effect on the two- and three-year-olds, but among the six- and seven-year-olds there immediately appeared what the author described as 'a really appreciable increase in interest, in spontaneity and in energy, and the quality of their building work'. The author concluded that by the age of six at least 90 per cent of children have well-developed competitive impulses which motivate them to perform better than they do when these competitive feelings are absent.

And so by the early nineteen thirties it had been found in both Germany and Austria that individual competitiveness acts as a motivation for work. About the same time it was discovered that this was also the case in the United States. The study was carried out by Maller at the Teachers' College at the University of Columbia.[6] He asked children to work arithmetic papers under two conditions. In the first, they wrote their names on the papers and were told that the papers would be marked and the best would get prizes. In the second, the children did the papers anonymously but were told that their class would be competing against other classes and the class which achieved the best overall mark would get a class prize. The result showed clearly that the children did better when they were working only for themselves. This is an important investigation because the motives being compared are not individual competitiveness versus no competitiveness, as in the studies in Germany and Austria, but individual competitiveness versus group competitiveness, and again individual competitiveness was shown to be a powerful motive.

Another important study was carried out in the United States about 1950 by Ausubel.[7] He took a group of children aged about twelve and gave them tests of arithmetical addition and letter cancellation. The tests were simple so that there would be no practice effect and the score would reflect the child's efforts. The arithmetic test consisted of eighteen pages of simple addition problems, and the cancellation test involved striking out every *e* in fourteen pages of prose. The task was to do as much as possible in a period of approximately half an hour.

The children first took the tests anonymously and a fortnight later they took duplicate tests competitively. It is worth quoting the actual instructions given to the children before they took the two tests. Here they are:

Anonymous session: 'The test that I am going to give you this morning is not the type of test that you are used to taking. I am not interested in the score which any one boy or girl makes. In fact, I will not know anybody's score, because I do *not* want you to put your names on your papers. I am only interested in finding out how fast boys and girls of your age can work with this type of material. Do you understand now why I am giving you this test?'

Competitive session: 'Two weeks ago, I gave you this same test to see how fast boys and girls of your age could work with this new material which you had never seen before. You did not have your names on your papers. Therefore, I could not tell how fast each one of you was working. Now that you have all had lots of practice with this type of material, we are going to do this test a little differently. This time we are going to have a speed contest. I want to find out who is the fastest worker in this class, the second fastest, third fastest, and so on down to the very slowest. The faster you work, the higher your score will be.

I will have your test marked by next week. Then I will prepare a list of your names, with each one's score next to his name. Your teacher will post this list on the bulletin board so that you will all be able to see how well you did on the test. Remember the faster you work the higher your score will be. Do you all understand the purpose of this test?'

Such were the instructions, and it can hardly be disputed that they spelt out clearly enough the two conditions for doing the tests. There were 79 children taking part in this experiment, and perhaps the reader would like to guess the number who did better in the second competitive test than in the first anonymous one. The answer: 79.

Notice that in this experiment the motivation compared with individual competitiveness is again different. Here it is altruism, since in the first session the children were being asked to help the psychologist in his investigation of how fast children can work, and this is compared with the children's motivation to achieve competitive success for themselves in the second session.

Such investigations as these demonstrate fairly conclusively that individual competition is an effective motive, but it has to be admitted that there are also progressive experiments designed to show that cooperation is more effective than competition. One of the most commonly cited is an investigation by Mintz.[8] What Mintz did was to take a wine bottle and fill it with a number of pellets attached to pieces of string which came out of the neck. Then he collected a group of children,

gave each of them one piece of string, and asked them to pull hard and see who could get his pellet out first. Thereupon every child pulled and all the pellets got jammed in the neck of the bottle. And so we see the kind of fiasco that arises when children compete, and if only they could cooperate sensibly and stop wanting to be first, they could form a queue and get all their little pellets out in a nice orderly fashion. This experiment is often cited in the more progressive textbooks of educational psychology to prove the superiority of co-operation over competition. It has, of course, no relevance to the question of how far children are motivated by competition.

However, it would be quite wrong to give the impression that the majority of authorities in educational psychology take the progressive position on the ineffectiveness of competition and the superiority of cooperation. On the contrary, most texts now take it as well established that individual competition is a powerful motivation for work. Two or three quotations should suffice to illustrate the position generally taken today. 'There is little doubt that competition operates as one of the outstanding incentives in school learning' (Blair, Jones and Simpson's *Educational Psychology*, 1967). 'Competition stimulates individual effort and productivity, promotes higher standards and aspirations, and narrows the gap between capacity and performance' (Ausubel's *Educational Psychology*, 1968). 'The evidence we have examined does not indicate that we should try to eliminate competition from the school' (De Crecco's *Psychology of Learning and Instruction*, 1968). These quotations are representative of the view taken of the value of competition as a motivation in leading contemporary texts.

Hitherto we have been concerned with experiments on competition in the sense of the drive to do better than others and there can be little doubt that this is a powerful motive for effort, work and achievement both in school and in life. But it is also possible to compete against some more general standard of excellence which is brought into play if a teacher tells a child that his work is good or bad. Here a child is being assessed against some rather vague and general criterion. This also motivates children. The motivating effects of both praise and reproof were established by Hurlock in an experiment where it was shown that children work better when they are given either praise or re-proof than they do when they are not told any-thing.[9] But it is probably not as effective as indi-vidual competition because it only mobilises a rather imprecise motive to do well and does not bring into play the motive of individual com-petitiveness against others in the same class or school.

From the work considered so far many people will no doubt draw the conclusion that the con-troversy over competition can now be allowed to rest. Evidently psychologists have demonstrated what common sense had already dictated, namely that children will work harder for success in competitive situations. It is desirable that children should work hard, and therefore it is sensible to strengthen the various forms of competition that mobilise competitive impulses such as marks, prizes, streaming, examinations and so forth. This, to many people, will seem the end of the matter. But we cannot expect that this will con-vince the progressive. He will move to other grounds, and it is to these other grounds that we shall now have to pursue him.

Effects of competition on the less able

One of the commonest arguments against com-petition lies in its adverse effects on the less able. Some children do well in competitions and that is all very well and pleasant for them, but others do badly and over the long term this builds up feelings of discouragement, rejection and aliena-tion. The progressive takes the view that this adverse effect of competition on the less able more than counter-balances its motivating effects on the more able, who are in any case more fortunately placed and quite able to look after themselves. Competition should therefore be abolished be-cause of its adverse effects on the less able.

Now this is a fair point and it is certainly impor-tant that every child and adult should have those feelings of self respect which come from being good at something and thereby contributing to the well-being of society. The answer to this point is that almost every child can be good at something and the problem has arisen only because of the over-academic bias of the secondary school curri-culum. For although almost every child can be good at something, only relatively few children

can be good at academic subjects, with their strong verbal component for which special verbal ability is necessary. This is abundantly obvious from common sense, since it is a matter of every-day knowledge that intellectuals who are good at academic school subjects by virtue of their high verbal abilities are often hopeless when it comes to mending household gadgets or repairing a car that has broken down. This diversity of special human aptitudes and abilities is not only evident from common sense but has been demonstrated in numerous investigations which show that there are only modest correlation coefficients between aca-demic abilities and mechanical aptitudes and skills.

The diversity of abilities among children is much wider than the relatively narrow range of verbal abilities tapped in the major part of the school curriculum. Indeed, it could be said that schools are run by people with high specific verbal ability for children with high specific verbal ability and that the rest who have other specific abilities, particularly in the area of mechanical aptitudes and practical skills, are discouraged by the system. This view cannot be pressed too far because general intelligence enters into all learning, but it contains a sufficient degree of truth to point to the solution of the problem that children who are less well endowed with verbal abilities get discouraged by the present school curriculum. The solution lies in the fact that almost everyone can be good at some subject, and the way to preserve self respect for everyone is not to abolish competition but to channel adolescents into the things they are good at. Then the boy who is good at car mechanics will have just as much self respect as the boy who is good at mathematics, and the girl who is good at graphic design will have just as much self respect as the girl who is good at French.

What is needed, therefore, is the introduction of many more vocational and practical subjects into the secondary school curriculum, including such things as the skilled machine tool crafts, the build-ing trades, motor mechanics and so forth. If there were this kind of choice, then almost everyone would find something which interested him and that he could be good at. Of course, the progres-sives' solution is the exact opposite of this. Their prescription is the common curriculum in the un-streamed comprehensive, designed to ensure that no one can be good at anything. Under this system all will then be equally ignorant and so a kind of equality is achieved, and no one feels the alienation that comes from failure although almost all will feel the alienation that comes from boredom and the absence of any sense of achievement. This is not the solution. We should think instead of the introduction of a much greater variety of choice of subject in the school curriculum, so that instead of no one being good at anything, everyone can be good at something, and achieve those feelings of self respect which come from doing something well.

That this is the right way to deal with this problem was to some extent realised many decades ago in the public schools. The masters apparently discerned that their charges could be divided broadly into swots and thugs, and so they devised two quite independent prestige areas consisting of academic work and games in which these two disparate types could compete. In this system even the dimmest tough could be good at some game and even the spottiest weed could be good at Greek. The idea was not sufficiently extended to practical skills, but as far as it went the principle was right and certainly more sensible than forcing all children to do the common curriculum as advocated today by progressive thinkers in education.

Probably a programme for an enlarged school curriculum with greater emphasis on mechanical and practical subjects as a means of overcoming the alienation of children with relatively poor verbal abilities would not incur the hostility of progressives to any considerable extent. Indeed, this position is quite similar to the progressive thesis that the educational system is a middle-class conspiracy to develop middle-class verbal abilities in children, particularly their own children, and thereby to keep the working class in a state of subservience. On this point progressive views and *Black Paper* views are probably quite close. That the mechanical and practical skills traditionally practised and possessed by the working class ought to be upgraded in terms of status, and no doubt financial reward also, in relation to middle-class verbal skills is precisely what the progressives have themselves been saying for some time. Here there is common ground. But this does not imply that competition is not a desirable means for the development of these diverse abilities.

Competition and cooperation

The progressive argument on competition moves now from school to society and takes the following form. Very well, the progressive will say, competition works, and it is possible to overcome the problem of the alienation of children with relatively poor verbal abilities by broadening the curriculum. But this does not mean to say that the use of competition in schools and the development and reward of competitive impulses are desirable. No doubt some people will strive to do better than others, no doubt ruthless ambition for self advancement is one of the great human driving forces, and no doubt children will work hard to get marks, and into the A stream, and so forth. But this is wrong. We don't want to encourage the development of this kind of person in our schools. This is just one of the unpleasant aspects of human nature which we should be doing our best to discourage as much as possible. Thus, although competition works, the progressive argues, competitiveness is not a desirable motive and it would be greatly preferable if schools could develop motivation to cooperate instead of motivation to compete.

The error in the progressive position here is to assume that we have to choose between competition and cooperation. The truth is that both are important. Let us admit straight away that the progressives are right in asserting the importance of cooperation and the development of cooperative attitudes in school children. Many occupations involve team work in which the members of the team must cooperate effectively to produce the product. A great deal of the world's work is done by cooperative teams, usually companies, and it is desirable for the members of these teams to have the ability, willingness and desire to cooperate. But these teams almost invariably have to compete against other teams. Where the progressives are wrong is in pitting cooperation against competition and in thinking that competition can be dispensed with and supplanted by cooperation. There is a need for both and a recognition that both are necessary.

The necessity to develop cooperative team attitudes as well as competitive ones has long been recognised in traditional educational practices. Cooperative attitudes have mainly been fostered through team games. The traditionalist view that it is difficult to develop cooperative attitudes in academic work is probably right, since there is something rather artificial about one class competing against another to see which can get the highest average in arithmetic. The reason for this is that academic work is almost entirely an individual and not a team activity, and the attempt to put it on a team basis does not carry conviction. The chief point is however that both competition and cooperation are necessary in life and that the skills and attitudes for both need to be developed in school children. The error of the progressives' position lies in their tendency to put exclusive emphasis on cooperation.

Competition in the modern world

We will now consider some of the implications of the progressive view that schools ought to educate children for a more cooperative form of society in which competition is reduced or eliminated. We have already seen that competitiveness is a powerful motive for the undertaking of effort and work, so that if the progressives were successful in significantly reducing individual competitiveness we should expect a concomitant reduction in the strength of people's motivation to work. There are some progressives who concede this and retort that work is no longer necessary. In the future work will be done by computers and machines, and humans will fill their time with play and, of course, sex. But here we are moving into realms of Utopian fantasy. Such a state of affairs may come about in the distant future but this is surely not close enough to begin preparing for by deliberately trying to reduce the competitive motivations of the present generation of school children.

Let us suppose that the progressives' programme for reducing competitive motivation in the population were successful and consider the implications for the country's economy and defence. Taking the economy first, the progressive argument is partly the conventional leftist one for more cooperative socialism and less competitive capitalism. But an attempt to implement this view of society comes up against severe practical constraints from Britain's position as a trading nation and the necessity to compete with other manufacturing nations to earn the currency to buy food and raw materials. For instance, if all the British car firms were nationalised and formed into a single state corporation, this would reduce competitiveness between the present British car firms, but the state car corporation would still have to compete in world markets against foreign car manufacturers. If the progressives were successful in reducing or eliminating competitive motivations so that the population simply didn't feel like competing any more, the consequence would surely be that the country would no longer be able to sell sufficient manufactured goods abroad to pay for imported food, some of the population might even die of starvation, leaving the rest to live on subsistence agriculture. This has been the experience of densely populated countries such as India and Bangladesh where the population for one reason or another cannot earn the foreign currency to buy food. There seems no reason why this could not happen in Britain if the progressive aim of eliminating the motivation to compete were to succeed. Before leaving national economic problems and their relation to national psychology, there is much to be said for the view that the British have been insufficiently competitive in the decades since the end of the Second World War, and that educationists would be better to try to increase the competitiveness of children rather than to reduce it.

But these are practical considerations and even if the progressive is willing to concede all the arguments hitherto advanced, he will probably still retain his view that in the ideal world cooperation should replace competition. In the imperfect real world of today it may be necessary to retain competitive impulses as motivation to work and for economic and military survival. But this is a pity, and in thinking about how society could be improved, we should as a long term goal try to work towards that ideal world where competition is replaced by cooperation.

This is one side of a controversy which has existed for centuries between those who see cooperative planning as the route to the ideal society and those who take the alternative position that the ideal society is more likely to arise through the gradual evolution of competing institutions and ideas by a trial and error process in which the more satisfactory survive and the less satisfactory are discarded. This alternative view is the philosophy of classical liberalism as formulated historically by John Locke, Adam Smith and J. S.

Mill, and which has been restated most comprehensively for the present generation by F. A. Hayek.[10] It is to this tradition and to its special application in education that the *Black Papers* belong. Perhaps the essence of the difference between the two philosophies lies in their estimation of the powers of the human mind. The progressive is more confident in these powers and the classical liberal less so. The progressive tends to believe that trained experts, no doubt assisted today by computers, can solve society's problems, and therefore that the most sensible thing is for experts to get together and plan cooperatively how society ought to be run. Thus trained economists will plan our economy, scientists will plan our science, and educationists will plan our schools. Classical liberals are less confident about human powers and less impressed by the abilities of experts. Their reading of history is that experts have so often been wrong that to leave them to plan cooperatively either in education or anywhere else would be to stifle progress.

On so many occasions advances seem to have come about not from the cooperative planning of experts but either unplanned and unforeseen, or seen dimly by some outsider who has turned out to be right. The best course is therefore to provide a framework in which a wide variety of different institutions and ideas will compete, and in the course of the competition the better will survive and the less good will be rejected. This is surely the way in which progress has generally come about. When a new idea is advanced it must necessarily compete with the existing ideas held by the current experts, as for instance when Copernicus proposed that the sun and not the earth was the centre of the solar system, as all the experts at the time supposed; or when Darwin proposed the evolution of species in place of the account given in Genesis. For a while the new idea has to compete with the traditional view and eventually the truth becomes clear.

Thus the essence of the argument that competition is desirable in principle is that human beings are not clever enough to produce in cooperation any single right answer. Fallible as we are, progress is more likely to come about from a diversity of competing ideas and institutions. Some of them will eventually prove to be better than others, but none of us is expert enough to tell for certain which those will be. This is why both in schools and in society generally the classical liberal favours diversity rather than uniformity, variety rather than equality, and competition between different ideas and institutions rather than cooperative central planning by experts. The application of this general principle to education leads classical liberals to welcome the existence of progressive schools even though they may be sceptical of the progressive methods practised in such schools. But we do not wish to close them down, as the progressives wish to close down the schools we favour, because we recognise that we could be wrong and therefore believe that progress in education, as elsewhere in society, is most likely to come about from competition between the widest variety of different types of school offering different methods and different curricula.

NOTES

1 A. Rowe in *Education for Democracy*, D. Rubinstein & C. Stoneman (Eds), Penguin Books, 1970.
2 J. Hemming in *The Red Paper*, Islander Publications, 1970.
3 H. C. Lindgren, *Educational Psychology in the Classroom*, J. Wiley, 1965.
4 W. Moede, *Experimentelle Massenpsychologie*, 1920, pp. 1–73.
5 P. J. Greenberg, 'Competition in Children', *American J. Psychol.*, 1932, 44, pp. 221–48.
6 J. B. Maller, *Cooperation and Competition: An Experimental Study in Motivation*, Teachers' College, Columbia University, 1929.
7 D. B. Ausubel, 'Prestige motivation of gifted children', *Genet. Psychol. Monogr.* 1951, 43, pp. 53–117.
8 A. Mintz, 'Non-adaptive group behaviour', *J. abnorm. soc. Psychol.* 1951, 46, pp. 158–9.
9 E. B. Hurlock, 'The value of praise and reproof as incentives for children', *Arch. Psychol.* No. 71, 1924, 11.
10 F. A. Hayek, *The Constitution of Liberty*, Routledge & Kegan Paul, 1960.

The University College at Buckingham

MAX BELOFF

When the Abbé Sieyès was asked what he had done during the reign of terror, he is said to have replied: 'J'ai vecu'. The answer was a fair one. The most important thing about an individual or an institution may be the sheer fact of survival. By far the most interesting, important (and surprising) thing about the University College at Buckingham is that it exists. It had a difficult birth and a dangerous infancy. Regarded with patent hostility by Mr Mulley and his political friends, cold-shouldered by the Committee of Vice-Chancellors and principals, narrowly avoiding strangulation in the cradle by the CNAA, subject to mockery and misrepresentation in much of the educational and intellectual press (thought unworthy of mention at any time by the *Economist*), its financial expectations eroded by depression and inflation, maddeningly confused in many people's minds with its neighbour the Open University, the College must, as it looks towards the end of its first year, be seen as something of a triumph of faith over probability. Those of us who work there daily, confronting the usual routine of teaching, timetables, classes, difficult students and impossible colleagues find it hard to believe at times that all this is really happening, and that the whole thing is not an invention of Kingsley Amis, Malcolm Bradbury, or some other Homer of campus wars.

Of course there are those who point out (and rightly) that what is actually being accomplished falls far short of what might have been thought of as possible in the lusher and more optimistic days of the nineteen-sixties. The College is not an institution that can make a contribution to Britain's problems in higher education of any quantitative significance; it is and will remain only a pilot plant. Production is another matter. Yet the existence of a pilot plant does justify the original belief that the state monopoly of higher education would (and sooner rather than later) develop some of the weaknesses of all monopolies, rigidity, bureaucracy, the *dis*economies of scale. Even with our limited size and tiny resources we can experiment and we can observe. Indeed observation may be more important than experiment, if only we can find time to set down and systematise our observations. It may well be that we shall come up with observations and experiments based upon them that none of us thought about when the idea was first mooted almost ten years ago.

It is probably that credit for having got this far is in very large part due to the sheer operation of chance—we found our original and generous benefactors by chance; we found our location at Buckingham, which has all in all proved a very favourable one, by another chance. We chose for one set of reasons to make law an important part of our offerings and thus came to profit for the time being by something quite different—the upsurge in the demand for legal education both here and overseas which meant that student recruitment (which was thought to be our major problem) has been relatively easy, with a guaranteed stream of good or goodish students in law while we find our feet and plan for more original and challenging branches of higher education.

On the other hand, we have been able to take advantage in different ways of a number of favourable currents in opinion in different quarters—the general swing of opinion away from the idea of the steady growth of state provision in all spheres at the expense of individual initiative and choice. But for that shift of opinion it would have been impossible to raise the necessary capital endowment from business firms and individuals themselves not particularly interested in, or clear about, purely educational objectives. Equally important has been the reaction among large sections of University teachers in many institutions and many disciplines against the constraints with which they battle, and a consequent determination to see that a new institution that may suggest some alternative ways of doing things is not allowed to go under for lack of encouragement and a variety of practical help. (The carping malevolence in officialdom seems as irrelevant to what actually happens when one seeks academic assistance or advice as are the would-be thunderbolts of the NUS to the attitudes of students one meets in the real world.) The same general goodwill has been found to exist in more than one profession. The handling of our affairs by the CNAA (Council for National Academic Awards) would indeed have proved fatal (since all our resources would have vanished long before we could have satisfied their regulations in a single field) had not the legal profession accepted the Buckingham licence as the equivalent of an honours degree for their professional purposes; if Universities had not been found to assure us that our students putting in for post-graduate places would not be discriminated against because they had a Buckingham licence rather than a bachelor's degree; and if employers has not been willing to say that what mattered was the tested quality of the individual job-seeker rather than the letters after his or her name. (I suppose the breakdown with the CNAA was the biggest piece of luck of all, since we can now see what we could not have known in advance, that all the experimenting we are doing and will want to go on doing would never be possible within their guidelines and subject to their constraints.)

Naturally we have also benefited by features of the British scene not designed for our benefit but very handy for our purposes. In the first place, the legal simplicity of the Companies Acts and of the requirements for charitable status means that it was relatively easy to find a legal framework for our operations not requiring the active participation of any public authority concerned with the merits or otherwise of the institution. It is the difficulty of finding such a framework that has frustrated to date all continental attempts to set up an institution of this kind. In the second place, the device of external examiners for the first degree means that there is no difficulty about monitoring our students' academic performance in a perfectly well understood fashion. The absence of such a convention in the much more heterogeneous American system has produced for new institutions problems of 'accreditation' which are less easily resolved. Thirdly, in Britain we are still in a post-imperial phase, which means that there are still a number of countries in which a period of British education is thought a respectable object of ambition so that while British schoolmasters (and still more British schoolmistresses) naturally inculcate a sense of caution in their charges, we have been able to fill vacant places with overseas students (not all of them of course from Commonwealth countries) some of them of high quality if presenting a variety of problems of their own. It is perhaps indicative that where we have found sympathy and help in Whitehall has been where departments are dealing with external affairs—in the Foreign and Commonwealth Office and the British Council.

So where do we stand now? We are coming, I think, to see that our specific contribution to the higher educational scene is to be found in at least four aspects of the College. It is and will remain a combination between the guiding ideas of the small American Liberals Arts college and the Oxbridge college in its classical form as above all an institution for the care of undergraduates. We have seventy students; we shall have a hundred and eighty next year (which means that we shall be twice as large as was my own Oxford college when I was an undergraduate in a literally antediluvian age). How rapidly we grow towards the target of 500 or so depends almost solely on the success of fund-raising for capital purposes. That may prove a long haul. The absence of State finance is not (as one might think) a guarantee of private liberality. Many of the foundations whose patronage of higher education is most trumpeted—and some famous firms—are far too keen to be in with the establishment, far too chary of acknowledging their own debts to the spirit of private enterprise, far too concerned with another knighthood or another life-peerage, or simply far too frequently advised by what I have come to think of as the 'pink mafia', those tame academics beloved of the powers-that-be who man all those committees and commissions, who make all those speeches in the House of Lords and whose business it is to conceal what every teacher knows to be true: the high price in quality we have paid for the form educational expansion has taken in this country in the last quarter century.

In the second place, the intensity of commitment which it was the purpose of our so-called two-year degree course to exemplify is clearly going to continue, and is, as one might expect, going to make a considerable impact on teachers and taught. Those who said one could not teach during the summer have been belied by our experience in a summer that no one could regard as exceptionally cool. It can be done.

In the third place, we are beginning to see how much is possible if one is prepared to take students as individuals and not as computer-fodder. We are more and more finding that good students can be found among candidates for admission who on paper look unusual or present problems (particularly on the linguistic side) that can be tackled in a student-oriented institution. We are rehabilitating teaching. In so far as Buckingham is beginning to exert a positive attraction rather than just being somewhere available, it is fairly clear that it is the impersonality of other institutions, particularly of some of the newer universities and the polytechnics, that is the thing that weighs with people.

In the fourth place, the degree to which an undergraduate education can be given an international dimension is obviously something which we are just beginning to probe. Sending our students to a special course at a French or German University in the interim period between leaving school and the beginning of our own academic year at the end of January which has been our most obvious innovation is only a beginning. Cooperation with European and American institutions can take and will take many different forms. Recruitment of staff (permanent and visiting) is being done, and successfully, on an international basis. An international student body has a somewhat less but still appreciably international group of teachers to cope with its problems. And it helps us to learn that there are other ways of doing things, and what things we do best here.

None of these four aspects of the College includes the experiments in what can constitute a liberal education in modern terms which one might hope will be the most important thing in the long run. Our school of Law, Economics and Politics is too small as far as the first year is concerned for an assessment of its educational value

to be made with any safety. The School of History, Politics and English Literature, our main newcomer for 1977, is still perforce on the drawing board. It is these schools rather than law (which much be largely conventional in structure) and even economics which deserve close monitoring. The Life Sciences have so far only a foothold to give a pointer towards the future.

What seems to be needed is a greater not a lesser willingness to see a first degree as preparation for a life of work that cannot always be satisfactorily foreseen by a young person of eighteen, and some questioning of what appears to be the practical lessons of current trends and manpower forecasting. The present pressure on places in law at Buckingham and elsewhere suggests a Britain (and for that matter a Nigeria) in which one half of the population will have to find reasons for litigation against the other half if the country is not to be engulfed in a flood of briefless barristers. The careers advisory office, which we shall (as promised) set up within the framework of our admissions office later this year, will have to engage to some extent in counter-suggestion.

It is of course argued in quarters unfavourable to the Buckingham venture that all that we do is vitiated because most of our students must be rich enough to pay their way. This criticism has some force though not for the reasons that the critics themselves would put forward. It is not true that the restriction largely to those who can pay means that we cannot get enough good students to fill our places. It is a vulgar illusion that the children of the well-to-do are likely to be less intelligent than the children of the less well-off. (It is true that great wealth may encourage idleness but against that there can be sanctions.) It is a fact however that some of our own students feel uncomfortable at the suggestion that they are in a privileged position, and would prefer to feel that they were part of a student body in whose selection financial considerations had played a lesser part. Much more important is the fact that unless the student body comes closer (at least in its British school-leaver element—our many mature students are special anyhow) to the general profile of the British student body at large, the value of Buckingham as a pilot plant is diminished. If our students come not so much from wealthier homes as from what goes with wealthier homes, more books, a travelled background and so on (not to speak of better sixth forms) it is hard to be sure whether any distinction of performance they show is due to what we provide rather than what they bring to us.

This situation can be and is being corrected. More local authorities are likely to follow the three pioneers—Devonshire, Lincolnshire and the London borough of Redbridge—in giving our students discretionary grants. More benefactors are coming forward with money for scholarships and bursaries. But it must be some time before the mix is what one would like it to be.

Meanwhile it is clear that much of what was said (and not only by our enemies) before we came into existence was misdirected. Our problems are often quite unexpected ones. What was nonsense (though it goes on being voiced) is the idea that we have escaped from the tutelage of the State only to succumb to the tutelage of business. A multitude of separate benefactors giving money often for quite different reasons is not a source of pressure. What is true in a fee-paying institution is that the customer (i.e. the student) has more of a voice and perhaps a more legitimate voice. My own hunch that 'student unrest' was the other face of student apathy and that both were the product of boredom through not enough being demanded of students looks like coming out correct. Our own students are neither bored nor (most of them) boring. They are very active, very demanding—sometimes impractically so—but that is one way of learning about the use of limited resources. Whatever else they learn, they will learn about time, space and money. One could do worse.

Marxism, knowledge and the academies

CAROLINE COX, KEITH JACKA AND JOHN MARKS

Nowadays in the academies of Britain—the institutions of higher education—there is continual and fundamental conflict.

Superficially the academies are quiet; they seldom make the headlines as they did a few years ago in the time of large-scale student occupation. But conflict now, especially among members of the teaching staff, is just as intense and more deeply grounded than at that time. Some would agree openly with this claim; others might sense the truth of it, but could not substantiate it.

The roots of the conflict lie deep in European cultural tradition and the clash has grown from a bifurcation and independent development of values which were originally shared.

Two groups are opposed in the conflict; we shall distinguish them as Academics and Marxists. 'Academics' because their way of thought and procedure (mode) has been gradually articulated and more or less established in the academies of Western Europe over a long period. 'Marxists', because they follow the doctrines of Karl Marx, and because many are members of Marxist political parties.

At the outset there is an unavoidable problem. Every sustained argument rests upon presuppositions concerning knowledge and truth, and these presuppositions will modify some aspects of presentation; but on these fundamental matters the two groups have radically different views. We therefore declare our commitment by stating that we write from within the Academic mode. We list some of the differences between this and the Marxist mode.

ACADEMIC MODE	MARXIST MODE

Extending knowledge

Inquiry is by individuals presumed free, i.e. uninhibited by the veto of persons or groups using extraneous (e.g. political) criteria. Choice of research topic is determined mainly by personal interest and the intellectual structure of the subject area.

'Freedom is the recognition of necessity.' Freedom as conceived by the Academics is 'bourgeois' freedom, i.e. a fraud or illusion. The writings of Marx (and usually those of other revered followers, e.g. Lenin, Stalin, Mao) are authoritative and their final interpreter is the Party, which reserves the right to guide the researcher directly.

Validating knowledge

Criteria are: logical coherence; use of all available relevant evidence. There is an open, critical and tentative attitude to knowledge; the style of argument and presentation is characteristically abstract, avoiding both emotional and moral pressure.

At all costs, results must be assimilated into a Marxist framework and again the Party has the final say. There is a dogmatic attitude to knowledge and Marxist analysis is claimed to be infallible. In controversy there are two distinct styles: formal and deductively sequential in accord with Marxist presuppositions; at other times, emotional, moralistic and pejorative when discussing work which is incompatible with Marxism.

Constitutions

Constitutionalism means limited government—limited by charters, rules and customs. Practitioners of this mode are committed to constitutionalism, some of them explicitly, and all of them implicitly.

Against constitutions. No limitation on the actions of the Party. Any profession of obedience to a constitution is superficial, expedient and transient.

Autonomy

Autonomy is valued both in respect of the institution as a whole, and in respect of individuals and departments within it.

No autonomy for individuals, departments or institutions.

Tolerance

Strong consensus on the value of pluralism and the importance of tolerance in an academy.

Pluralism and tolerance are 'bourgeois' and both are despised. Extreme intolerance of opponents, which may be moderated by expediency when practitioners are not in control.

Morality, custom, tradition

No consensus. A wide range of attitudes. Some followers of traditional morality, with a clear belief in moral imperatives; some lukewarm; some

Marxism is intensely moralistic, but yet there are no moral imperatives. Morality has no independent existence apart from material interests and is outright immoralists who claim their individual right to examine all customs and moral positions on their merits and to act accordingly.

theoretically immanent in the proletariat (in practice, this means the Party, the 'Organised Vanguard of the Proletariat'). The Party can therefore do no wrong and everything is permitted in opposing 'bourgeois ideologists'. Custom and traditional morality are shackles of the past to be thrown aside in the transition—both inevitable and desirable—from Capitalism to Socialism.

Articulateness and aggression

Better at practising the academic mode than explicating it. Usually inept in controversy with Marxists and prefer to avoid conflict.

Well versed in their beliefs and given to proselytising. Recognise the conflict with the academic mode and ceaselessly attack it, directly or indirectly. Persistent hatred of liberalism.

The Academic mode is complex, but relatively easy to describe, because there is no conscious attempt at deception. With the Marxists, as with all totalitarian movements, the situation is less clear because self-presentation is carefully predetermined, varying both with their strength and with the audience. When weak, they underplay their distinctiveness and radicalism; when strong, they speak more as they believe. They address themselves to four kinds of audience: general public, sympathisers, outer party, inner party. When addressing the furthest circle—the general public—Marxists speak entirely expediently: there may be no relation between words and intention. Frankness increases the more one approaches the centre. All of this makes accurate deduction difficult.

What is manifest in the Marxist mode is a well-defined but, by older standards, peculiar attitude to truth. If insight and morality, hence truth and the telling of it, are exclusive to a social group; if truth is a property which has a historically mobile existence and in our epoch resides in the proletariat—especially its 'organised vanguard', the Party; then all Party statements are unquestionable and statements from non-Party-members have no standing. Familiar standards of truth and falsehood do not apply. A similar analysis applies to those other totalitarians of our time, the Nazis, with the Aryan race substituting for the proletariat. This style is characteristic of modern totalitarianisms, combining fanatical moralism with extreme cynicism.

For simplicity of presentation we have ignored factions amongst Marxists. This matters little because:

(a) In opposition to the Academics they present an effectively united front.

(b) Marxism is essentially monolithic, anti-pluralist. Factions are not accepted as permanent. In states with a Marxist government only one party is permitted.

Mixed mode

Until recently the practitioners of the Academic mode were clearly dominant in societies such as Britain. They constituted the establishment. There were some Marxists, but nowhere in large numbers, and although many were quite open about their beliefs they made no attempt to change the procedures of the institutions in which they worked. Hence arose the common opinion that the Marxists of earlier decades were liberal at heart. We suggest that subsequent changes in the ways in which many Marxists operate are superficial, and due mainly to changes in relative proportions.

Because times *have* changed. In the seventies there are departments where Marxists form a majority of the staff and can therefore speak and act according to the full rigour of their beliefs. Along with this change there has developed a hybrid or *Mixed mode*. Practitioners of this mode are eclectics: they treat the two modes we have summarised as aggregates of elements, rather than recognising them as two fundamentally incompatible systems. Therefore, their attempts to select various elements from each, to make up a hybrid aggregate of explanation and procedure, are inevitably flawed by inconsistencies. In certain areas of scholarship, particularly in the social sciences, this group is more numerous than either of the two original ones. We shall explain later why we think that the deep inconsistencies of this new mode operate effectively to strengthen the Marxists and to weaken the Academics.

Alternatives

Faced with this situation of conflict, the member of the academic staff has many alternatives. Our discussion will refer, directly or by implication, to three of them.

1 To practise a mixed mode.
2 To become a dogmatic hard-line supporter of one of the two main modes.
3 To choose one of the main modes but, recognising its inadequacies, to try to reform it so as to remove them.

In this essay we shall be arguing in favour of a reformed version of the Academic Mode. We consider that the two main modes are incompatible and incommensurable; there is no possible compromise between them in relation to the crucial matters of truth, knowledge and validation. We therefore reject any eclectic position. We reject also the Marxist world-view as one which contains certain basic intellectual errors. These errors are so central that to eliminate them would be to make the word 'Marxist' no longer applicable. We believe that the Academic mode as usually practised also contains important intellectual errors, but that reform is possible without changing it beyond recognition.

Theory and values

We have said that most practitioners of the Academic mode are inept at articulating or justifying their typical procedures. In a time of conflict this is a serious weakness. The necessary minimum of agreement on theory and values would cover:

(a) a substantial part of a theory of knowledge;
(b) parts of a theory of society, and some related social practices;

(c) some elements of a theory of morality, and certain moral values.

(a) is obvious since the primary purposes of an academy include the extension, transmission and preservation of knowledge, and the provision of training in advanced skills;

(b) accords with the fact that only certain kinds of society will permit the practice of the Academic mode;

(c) follows from the fact that the Academic mode contains a large number of (mostly implicit) moral presuppositions. (The most obvious ones relate to honesty and tolerance.)

In each of these fields—knowledge, society, morality—we consider that there is a range of doctrines and procedures which are compatible with the Academic mode; whereas outside the range there is incompatibility. We shall not attempt the difficult task of trying completely to delimit these ranges, but we will first outline particular theories of knowledge, society and morality which we support, and each of which we believe to lie within the compatible range. We shall then indicate aspects of Marxism which locate it outside this range.

Knowledge

Implicitness We recognise a familiar human face by the whole, not by the parts. And yet it must be true that in some way we know the elements of that face, else we could not distinguish it from others. As children we learn to speak effectively without explicit knowledge of the language we are using. We grasp the meaning of a mathematical theory in use, after we have internalised it, made it part of ourselves. This is the structure of all recognition, learning and comprehension. Every act of knowing of an entity includes necessarily these implicit internalised elements which we build and rely upon—take for granted. One could say that we attend *from* these implicit elements in order to attend *to* what we are concerned with. We reject then as inconceivable the ideal of a completely *explicit* knowledge.

Personality Knowledge is held by a person, not by a book or a computer. A book contains marks on paper which lead to knowledge in the mind of a person who reads. Since a person and his actions are unique, knowledge is, in practice and to a limited extent, itself unique to that person. But there are, of course, a vast number of common elements of knowledge amongst persons, and all language and communication is based on this. Much of our most important learning is more inextricably personal than even the above would suggest; because typically we learn complex skills in an interpersonal way, by identifying—feeling, imitating, thinking—with another *person* who already knows. Strictly, then, there is no such thing as completely detached, impersonal knowledge. Such adjectives must be used with care if they are not to be misleading.

Authority In most of our learning we rely on authority. A child babbles, imitates and gradually learns language by relying on the potential meaningfulness of the sounds made by his parents. A student learns the language of algebra, which at first seems gibberish, by a similar belief in its potential meaning. He trusts in the authority of his teacher and believes before he knows. By the time we are adult each of us possesses a large amount of knowledge, a little of which we have verified, some of which we have learnt unaided, but most of which we have acquired with the aid of authorities.

Reality Knowledge is of reality. We presume the existence of a reality greater than ourselves, which we relate to in the act of knowing. The nature of this independent reality will underlie and constrain our claims to knowledge, but will also make it possible for different persons to grasp reality in similar ways; it is in this respect that knowledge can be objective. However, since reality is inexhaustibly complex, our knowledge of it will inevitably be incomplete and tentative.

Levels and irreducibility Knowledge is achieved by attending from internalised details to the meaningful whole, and is therefore based on and constrained by these details. There is a correspondence between the structure of an act of knowing with its two aspects (implicit details and meaningful whole) and the structure of an entity which can be known. Consider a machine whose parts (corresponding to the implicit details) are constrained by the laws of physics and chemistry. So it will eventually wear out, according to the processes of friction, chemical corrosion, etc. Also these laws rule out certain possibilities, such as a perpetual motion machine.

The meaning of the machine (corresponding to the meaningful whole in knowing) is revealed in the purpose for which it was shaped. A new concept has emerged, that of design for a purpose, using objects as instruments. This is the central concept of technology, not describable within the terms and laws of physics and chemistry, and therefore in this sense a *non-reducible* concept. The new principle—in this case, design—operates at a higher level, by selecting one out of the many possibilities left undetermined by the lower level. (Physics and chemistry do not prescribe the shapes of lumps of metal, which we are therefore free to mould as we please.)

A similar analysis could be made of other irreducible principles.

For this paper we do not need an evolutionary theory of emergence of these higher principles. It is enough if it is agreed that they exist, are recognisable, and are irreducible.

Those who disagree do so in one of two ways. There are those who deny irreducibility. These are the reductionists, who emphasise constraint, claiming that life is entirely explicable in terms of physics and chemistry, or that justice is merely a mystifying way of describing the will of the stronger, or that true freedom is the recognition of necessity. The other group denies constraint. These are the perfectibilists (absolutists, transcendentalists, millenarians) who chafe at any material limitation on love, or rage at the smallest evidence of less than perfect justice in the world.

Morality

Morality is an aspect of persons and is constrained by all those levels which underlie the existence of persons. In particular, morality operates through personal actions involving choices among the many possibilities left open by the lower level constraints of self-preservation and self-interest. Morality is in the making; it is not fully emerged. Many people recognise implicitly that there are universal moral principles—most obviously, although not only, in close personal relations—but are yet not satisfied with attempts to explicate them. It is consistent to hold that such principles exist and that our awareness of them has evolved slowly while still maintaining a tentative attitude to current efforts at explication. The parallels with claims to knowledge are clear.

Society

An order such as a motor-car, a factory, an army, was designed with one or several purposes in mind. It is an instrument of human will. We shall describe such a designed order by the words *organisation* and *machine*. On the other hand a plant, an animal, a language, a society are orders which were not designed. They are *self-generating* orders which evolved, and the ideas of design and purpose do not apply. (Because an order—e.g. a language—helps in satisfying certain human needs it does not follow that it was designed for the purpose of satisfying those needs.)

Note that not all orders fall clearly into one or other of these classes.

Constructive rationalism is a view which has been dominant in European social thought for the last three hundred years. It is reductionist, ignoring or blurring the distinction between the two kinds of order, implying that the machine is the correct and complete model for understanding any order. The intellectual fathers are Descartes and Hobbes, both of whom explained man by analogy with a machine; the latter explained society also by using this model.

Evolutionary rationalism insists on the distinction between the two orders, especially in understanding man and society. Man is seen as a rule-following animal, quite as much as a purposive one, and human culture as partly an order of rules which we inherit, and only partly as an order of rules which have either been designed or fully explicated. Many rules have evolved, been strengthened and refined by selection. Man has often been successful because he observed rules, not because he understood why he did so. It is not in any way irrational to follow rules we do not clearly understand. (Even now we have only a small understanding of the structure of a language.) The evolution of social rules and institutions is as important for understanding man and society as is biological evolution for understanding man as a species. Knowing this, one can appreciate more accurately the potential benefits and limitations of conscious design, and one is better placed to distinguish those situations where the constructive rationalist model will be most fruitful. A complex self-generating order of individuals, institutions and organisations, which is a modern society, makes continual use of constructive rationalism in limited areas, but in its totality such a society bears little resemblance to a machine.

Marxist mode: the wider setting

We now have the essential apparatus for a more thorough exposition and criticism of the Marxist mode.

Marxism is a programme of radical social change associated with a world view which explains succinctly all human history, conflict, culture and mental life. Its ideas come mainly from Marx, and its methods and organisation mainly from Lenin, who however only spelt out what was clearly implied in many of Marx's writings.

(a) It is millenarian. Man is perfectible, and the way to perfection—perfect justice, equality, fraternity; an end to the exploitation of man by man—is by a radical change of society.

(b) The struggle of social classes is the mainspring of history. Theoretically, in the present epoch the locus of energy, intelligence and morality is the proletarian class.

(c) The best way to change society radically is by creating a Communist Party which will rightly engross to itself all political and social power. The Party embodies the will of the proletariat.

(d) The mode of production—i.e. the kind of economy: feudal, capitalist, socialist—is the primary determinant of all aspects of social, political, cultural and intellectual life.

This is the official theory of modern Marxist Parties, and it accords quite closely with practice as observed over a long period in the USSR and in both Eastern and Western Europe.

For all its simplicity, constructive rationalism was for a long time an exceedingly fruitful view, both in intellectual life and in social reform. One of its effects was to help to weaken and finally destroy the authority of the Church over large sections of the population. And this let loose the Utopian social aspirations which until then had been contained within the Church. Marxism was one of the movements which inherited and redirected those aspirations. It did this by combining them with a structure of explanation which is an extreme version of constructive rationalism. To see this, let us consider the characteristics of a good machine:

It is an instrument, well-designed for its purpose.

It is unified and harmonious.

Each element has a function and all are interdependent.

It is entirely knowable and describable by its designer.

In improving the design of a machine one does not hesitate to refashion certain elements, and to discard redundant parts.

Each of these characteristics is reflected in the Marxist explanation of society and its proposals for perfecting society by redesigning it, which are as follows:

The purpose of society is to realise the ideals of justice, equality, fraternity.

Received tradition, customary morality and authority are relics of the past. They are seen as bemused attempts at achieving certain purposes, and/or deliberate mystification by particular interest groups wishing to impose their own design on society.

Since a well-designed society is unified, harmonious and easily knowable, demands for personal independence, institutional autonomy and intellectual pluralism are either misguided or sinister. Obviously only one political party should exist; also government and society should be completely interdependent. Within such a system the idea of an autonomous academy is merely ridiculous. The prime mover of society is the Party. This is also the re-designer, the improver of the social machine, and does not hesitate to refashion certain elements (re-education to dissipate 'false consciousness') or to discard (liquidate) redundant or frictional elements (kulaks, aristocrats, religious believers, strikers, etc.)

Marxism is a typical modern movement in that it is at the same time reductionist (in relation to society) and perfectibilist (in its claims for the future moral order). It is arbitrary, and intellectually weak in its simplistic grounding of institutions and mental life essentially in the mode of production. But the centre piece is its doctrine of the Party. This results inevitably in the collapse of all social hierarchies except that of power, the concentration of this power in the hands of a tiny minority, and the disfranchising of all other persons in the economic, political, intellectual and moral realms.

Since validation of truth rests with the Party there will be direct and indirect control regarding the extension and transmission of knowledge, by persons whose own knowledge will inevitably be limited and whose first criterion will be the preservation of their own power. At times they will be driven to ignore boundary constraints of lower level realities (Soviet agricultural policy); they will be driven to distort facts in the most extreme way (the spectacular variations in successive editions of Soviet works of reference); they will suppress emergent movements in art and science; they will attempt to eliminate ethnic and religious groups who challenge the Party's ideological hegemony.

This violation of natural constraints and the inhibiting of evolutionary emergence (with its associated potential of diversity and adaptability) can be expected to weaken the ultimate survival capacity of a Marxist society.

Academic mode: the wider setting

The Academic mode is based on the distinction between the individual and the reality in which he exists. To survive he must try to understand this reality, but since it is complex and inexhaustible his attempts to make sense of it will always be partial and may be mistaken. Honest claims to knowledge, therefore, however boldly presented, will still be open and tentative, and one who truly wants to know will support investigative freedom for all and will welcome a plurality of schools of thought and points of view. Thus liberal values and attitudes (openness, tentativeness, pluralism and individual freedom) are intimately linked with efforts to know the external world and to adapt to it.

The social system of the academic world, evolved in accord with all this, attempts to lessen the disadvantage of each individual's having only a partial and finite view. The core of the system is its structure of collective validation. Claims are initiated by individuals, but they operate within the constraints of both authority and the collective judgement of a group of peers. But the structure is ultimately grounded in logic and evidence, and these primary criteria are freely acknowledged by all members of the academic community. In this way the whole community can generate and use a vastly greater stock of collectively validated knowledge than any individual or centralised group could possibly do.

Likewise we suggest that since modern complex societies make use of a huge array of knowledge, they need to foster a range of values and procedures similar to those of the academic world (pluralism, individual freedoms, easy access to information). In liberal societies these values and procedures operate within a system of collective constraints—especially legal and ethical ones—which have partly evolved spontaneously and only partly been designed. There is thus a deep affinity between the Academic mode and the kind of liberal society which seems best able to nurture it, and also an affinity between the two principal functions of the academy. And there is an obvious disharmony between the Academic mode and any society where the government (or church) insists on complete control of all institutions of information. These characteristics of liberal decentralised societies are related to their capacity for adaptive change which seems to be (as one would expect) much greater than that of centralised societies.

The Academic mode under attack

The core of the academy consists of: a set of procedures centred on the validation of knowledge, an implied view of what knowledge is, and the necessary additional elements from social theory and ethics. The Marxists attack this core and those who would preserve it.

The academy will withstand this attack more or less strongly to the extent that:
(a) Procedures are effective and well-matched with the main purposes of the academy.
(b) The proportion of members who willingly practise these procedures is large or small.
(c) Such members can sincerely and coherently justify the procedures, and themselves think and act in ways consistent with the principles underlying these procedures.

We have argued already that (a) is a correct summary—procedures *are* effective and well matched. Of (b) it is enough to say that these persons—the practitioners of the Academic mode—still exist in large numbers. (c) points to the trouble spot; this description fits very few people in the academies.

Instead it will happen that an able academic,

accepting appreciatively the authority structures of his scholarly specialism, will yet openly denigrate the principle of authority in other contexts. Another scholar will boldly define himself as an immoralist, conveniently forgetting how much in practice, both inside and outside the academy, he relies upon such moral values as honesty and tolerance. A man like this may well collapse when faced with the thorough-going immoralism of the Marxists.

Typically in the same person an unreflective reductionism in presenting theories of knowledge, society and morality will be conjoined with a practice which is much more subtle and more in accord with the quite different notions of evolutionary rationalism.

The Mixed mode increases the confusion. Its practitioners often do not see that they use two incompatible sets of criteria for the validation of knowledge and so are unaware of thereby shaking the foundations of both. But the Marxists withstand this more easily than the Academics since Marxism depends as much on emotion and moral perfectibilism as on reason.

As one would expect, from their parallel evolution and shared values of tolerance and pluralism, there are other institutions of a liberal society which are vulnerable to attack in much the same ways as its academies, especially to attack by internal intransigent groups, however small.

Marxism: strength and weakness

Marxism teaches that only via its precepts can humanity achieve its full economic and cultural potential and create a form of society based on justice, equality and fraternity. But reality is recalcitrant. Only through the intricate structures of modern complex societies, including the academies, can Marxism try to realise these dreams. And we have argued that there is an inevitable conflict between the ways in which such societies function, especially in regard to knowledge, and the methods which Marxism does and must employ: detailed central control of all cultural, political and social life, covering therefore all aspects of information and education.

So that when Marxists gain power and make theirs the official doctrine of a state, there develops a great gulf between promise and performance—nowhere so spectacular as in the moral realm. Documentation is most complete and scholarly for the USSR.

On justice, consider the promises clearly implied in the extremely liberal Soviet Constitution of 1936, coupled with the facts of the show trials and the great purges. Fraternity is annihilated when an organ of government, the security police, is ordered to engage in systematic terror and mass murder. It is the elite of the Party itself—the new class—who benefit most from inequality; their great economic and social privileges are officially guaranteed. In applied science, consider the damaging effects on Soviet agriculture of Party interference in biology (the Lysenko affair).

This extreme gap between promise and performance is potentially damaging to the Marxist cause. It increases the need to control all information and generates intellectual strategies of concealment which, although they vary in emphasis, are common to Marxists of all countries. These strategies aim to turn all the forces of critical thought and social reform against Western liberalism. In comparative analysis of societies Marxists will carefully select from the evidence, ignoring uncomfortable facts about Marxist societies and concentrating on the iniquities of capitalism. They pre-empt whole areas of investigation with loaded concepts like 'bourgeois imperialism', and try to capture for their exclusive use words such as 'critical' and 'radical'. They play down the importance of non-social constraints on human behaviour (e.g. biological constraints, or those from the physical world).

Along with other totalitarians, Marxists genuinely hate liberalism: because a perceptive liberal could call their bluff, and because a liberal society reaches levels of achievement which are inherently beyond the reach of Marxism.

The current Marxist strategy for bringing down liberal societies concentrates on winning preponderant influence in key institutions (schools and academies are particularly important). Their tight discipline offsets lack of numbers. They use the methods of modern propaganda, especially the device of endless reiteration; they try to place committed young Marxists in key positions in society—here the academies are particularly useful as indoctrination and training grounds, and as distribution centres; and they multiply their effectiveness by creating front organisations, enlisting

support from the much larger number of persons who think of themselves as liberals.

The intellectual poverty and moral fraudulence of Marxism, and the enormous energy spent in concealing these qualities, reveal weakness rather than strength. And skilful organisation alone would not neutralise this weakness. None the less Marxism in practice is formidable. Its appeal and strength become clear if we consider what exactly mature Marxism has proved to be, namely, a perfectibilist cult manipulated by a new class in order to win, and hold, power.

Modern man is just as perfectibilist and gullible as his ancestors, except that now the dreams relate more to the moral than the material realm. An academy is particularly vulnerable, because it must remain an open institution, and because there is a fine dividing line between a realistic exploratory imagination and one swayed by Utopian fantasies.

BIBLIOGRAPHY

Many of the fundamental ideas we outline are discussed in:

1 M. Polanyi, *The Tacit Dimension*, Routledge & Kegan Paul, 1967.
2 F. A. Hayek, *Law, Legislation and Liberty*, Vol. 1, Routledge & Kegan Paul, 1973.

Much evidence concerning the situation in the Soviet Union, both past and present, is given in:

3 L. Shapiro, *The Government and Politics of the Soviet Union*, Hutchinson, 1973.
4 A. Solzhenitsyn, *The Gulag Archipelago*, Vols 1–3, Collins/Harvill, 1974–6.
5 A. Sakharov, *My Country and the World*, Collins/Harvill, 1975.

The conflict in West German academies has been analysed and documented in detail in the following articles; this situation has not been well reported in this country and deserves to be better known.

6 H. Schelsky, 'The Wider Setting of Disorder in the German Universities', *Minerva*, Vol. X, No. 4, October 1972, pp. 614–26.
7 W. Ruegg, 'The Intellectual Situation in German Higher Education', *Minerva*, Vol. XIII, No. 1, Spring 1975, pp. 103–20.
8 J. Domes and A. Frank, 'The Tribulations of

the Free University of Berlin', *Minerva*, Vol. XIII, No. 2, Summer 1975, pp 183–99.

Finally, for much significant information on Communist tactics in their world-wide attempts to gain power, see:

9 T. T. Hammond (Ed), *The Anatomy of Communist Takeovers*, Yale University Press, 1975.

10 C. Cox, K. Jacka, J. Marks, *The Rape of Reason*, Churchill Press, 1975.

VALUES

Questions

1 Are children, as A. S. Neill wrote in Summerhill, 'innately wise and realistic'?

2 Is it natural or unnatural for teachers and parents to tell children what to do?

3 Is a child under thirteen years of age ready to decide what activities are worth pursuing at school?

4 Are children happiest in an orderly or disorderly classroom?

5 In a society dominated by pop culture, do children need more, or less direction by concerned adults?

6 Will children work hard in a non-competitive atmosphere? At languages? At mathematics? At football?

7 How much Marxist indoctrination is taking place in schools, colleges, polytechnics and universities?

8 How far are social workers applying Marxist doctrines in their daily work?

9 Should a teacher treat children as individuals in their own right instead of seeing them (and himself or herself) as a product of class struggle?

10 How can the desire of the public, particularly parents, that schools should continue to teach the Christian religion and the values of a democratic society be put into practice?

Contributors

R. T. Allen taught English for four years at a grammar school. He is now lecturer in Education, Loughborough College of Education.

R. W. Baldwin has been Chairman of the Governors of Manchester Grammar School since 1965, and co-opted Member of Manchester Education Committee, 1967–71. He was with the Board of Trade from 1935 for 13 years, and became Assistant Secretary. In 1948 he left to go into the cotton industry.

Geoffrey Bantock recently retired as Professor of Education, University of Leicester.

Jacques Barzun was until recently the University Professor at Columbia, New York. His book *The House of Intellect* has become famous as a critique of progressive education.

Max Beloff is Principal, University College of Buckingham.

Rhodes Boyson, ex headmaster, Highbury Grove School, is now MP for Brent North.

Caroline Cox has been Head of the Sociology Department at the Polytechnic of North London since 1974. She has been a nurse in the East End. With Keith Jacka and John Marks (see below) she was author of the famous *The Rape of Reason*.

C. B. Cox is Professor of English at the University of Manchester.

H. J. Eysenck is Professor of Psychology, University of London Institute of Psychology.

Stuart Froome, ex headmaster of St Jude's Church of England School, Englefield Green, was a member of the Bullock Committee.

Keith Jacka taught mathematics at the Polytechnic of North London.

Alfred Levy is senior teacher in charge of mathematics at an East London comprehensive. He has had 13 years as a primary school teacher, followed by 16 years as a specialist in a secondary school.

Ron Lewis is a Senior Probation Officer, and has held office at local, regional and national level in the National Association of Probation Officers.

Richard Lynn is Professor of Psychology, New University of Ulster.

John Marks lectured for two years at a Swedish university before moving to the Polytechnic of North London in 1966 where he teaches Physics. Member of the Labour Party.

Patrick Moore, free-lance author, has written more than sixty books, mainly on astronomy, and is particularly well-known for his radio broadcasts and television appearances.

E. R. Norman is Dean and Chaplain of Peterhouse, Cambridge, and university lecturer in Modern British History. He is a member of the Standing Committee of the National Society for Religious Education.

John Price taught for many years in London's East End, has an honours degree in science and is now headmaster of Walderslade Boys School, Chatham.

Stuart Sexton will be fighting Burnley for the Conservatives at the next election. He is a Councillor, and a member of Croydon Education Committee.

R. G. A. Sherratt is music teacher at Thomas Alleyne's High School, now a comprehensive.

Renee Soskin has been since 1970 headmistress and owner of Bury Lawn School, an independent co-educational day school in Newport Pagnell, Bucks. She was on the staff and Governing Body of King Alfred School, London, for many years. She has been well-known as an active Liberal.

Robert Vigars has been from 1974 Leader of the Opposition, Inner London Education Authority. He is a solicitor, and has made frequent radio and television broadcasts on London politics.

Dolly Walker took her Froebel Diploma in 1956 as a mature student when already a mother of two school-age children. She was remedial reading teacher at William Tyndale for $5\frac{1}{2}$ years, and now teaches at Dulwich College Preparatory School for Boys.

Stephen Woodley is head of the English Department at the King's School, Canterbury. He is also a member of the Kent Education Committee.